Old Tyne

from Throckley to Walker

John and Drew Edminson

© John and Drew Edminson 2002
First published in the United Kingdom, 2002,
by Stenlake Publishing
Telephone / Fax: 01290 551122

ISBN 1 84033 214 X

FURTHER READING

The books listed below were used by the authors during their research. None of them are available from Stenlake Publishin
Those interested in finding out more are advised to contact their local bookshop or reference library.

Bean, David, *Tyneside, A Biography*, 1971

Bennison, Brian, *Lost Weekends: A History of Newcastle's Public Houses*, 1998

Benwell CDP, *Whatever Happened to Council Housing?*, 1976

Canneux, T. P. and Hanson, N. H., *The Trolleybuses of Newcastle upon Tyne 1935–1966*, revised edition, 1985

Davies, Peter and Maile, Ben, *First Post: From Penny Black to the Present Day*, 1990

Fairley, Peter, *Images of Tyneside*, 1995

Foster, Joan, *Newcastle upon Tyne, A Pictorial History*, 1995

Graham, Frank, *Newcastle Quayside, Sandhill, Side and Clos* 1991

Hearse, George, *Tramways of Northumberland*, 1961

Joyce, J., *Roads and Rails of Tyne and Wear 1900–1980*, 1985

Manders, Frank, *Bygone Central Newcastle*, 1995

Michael, Liz, *Bygone Walker*, 1992

Stabler, Arthur, *Gannin' alang the Scotswood Road*, 1997

The lady window cleaners of Newcastle.

Front cover illustration: Looking across the Swing bridge to Newcastle from the Gateshead side in the 1920s.

Back cover illustration: This photograph was taken at Newcastle Central station in 1903. Constructed that same year Newcastle Corporation Tramways, car No. 93 was one of the first trams to be built for the city's network. It had eight whe and an uncanopied upper deck and could travel at a maximum speed of 12 mph, which was considered fast in its day. By mid-1930s trolleybuses were beginning to replace the trams and on 4 August 1951 the last tram rolled into Gateshea Sunderland Road depot.

INTRODUCTION

is possible to trace the history of settlement on the Tyne to
veral thousand years before the arrival of the Romans, when
steeply sloping site ten miles from the river's mouth was
osen as a place to inhabit. This site grew to become
ewcastle. It was an ideal position for fortification, and when
e Romans arrived 1,900 years ago they could see the
raction of the location too.

The first bridge to span the Tyne was the Roman-built *Pons
lius*, constructed in the time of Emperor Hadrian in AD 122.
fort and small harbour were built alongside the new bridge,
nich was located at the lowest possible crossing point of
e Tyne. The site is now occupied by Lord Armstrong's 1876
ving bridge. Tyneside remained under Roman occupation
r the next 300 years until the early 400s. By this time
ewcastle's foundations had been laid, and evidence of the
st commercial activity on Tyneside had been recorded.

For the next 600 years there is scant information of activity
the area, though it is believed that some limited habitation
d trading took place between AD 875 and 1070 when a group
monks settled on the banks of the Tyne. Their new home
ok the name of Monkchester.

If the early stages of Newcastle's development were rather
w and uneventful, then the year 1080 marked a major
rning point. Having subdued Malcolm III of Scotland in
72, William the Conqueror visited the Tyne and instructed
eldest son, Robert Curthose, to build a motte and bailey
stle which was completed eight years later. This *Novum
stellum* gave the city the name by which it has been known
the last 900 years, New-castle.

This particular spot on Tyneside was chosen because of its
ategic location; the towering new structure was intended
act as both a deterrent against civil insurrection within
gland and a defence against the unruly Scots. A stone keep
s added during the reign of Henry II in 1178.

In the fourteenth century, still conscious of the threat posed
the Scots, funds were raised through a murage (levy) to
ild the town walls, and when constructed they rivalled
ose of any English city. With the walls came added security
ich led to increased commercial activity and trade,
owing Newcastle to flourish.

For the next 400 years Tyneside experienced a rather
remarkable period in its history, with the exception of the
ruption of Scottish occupation in the 1640s, brought about
the early events of the English Civil Wars. However, by
1800s a number of major factors were coming into play
ich significantly transformed the area and began to create
classical city of Newcastle as recognisable today.

In national terms, the North-East was a late industrialiser,
t in terms of its nature, scale and overall dominance it
ayed a highly significant part in the Industrial Revolution.
combination of the finest transport links with the south
ough rail and sea, and a wealth of natural resources made
neside one of the cornerstones of the Industrial Revolution.
ack gold' beneath the ground was the most important asset.
e North-East coalfield was the largest in the world and in
mid-nineteenth century coal was the principal source of
el for both industrial and domestic use. The need to
nsport coal plus other goods and materials gave rise to
Tyne's second most important industry, shipping. A great
mber of extremely famous vessels have been launched
m the Tyne docks, several of which are featured in this
ok.

In addition to excellent natural resources and transport
links, Tyneside had one other often overlooked but major
factor in its industrial growth, its people. Just as today,
nineteenth century Geordies were hardy, adaptable, good-
humoured folk, capable of meeting every challenge.

In the 1830s Newcastle's vastly increased wealth, rising
population, industrial growth and more sophisticated
commercial background made it essential to develop a new
town centre which could house the necessary shops, offices
and buildings demanded by such a community. Various
plans were submitted to the town council, and it was left to a
group of talented speculators to transform Newcastle and
leave their legacy. The famous names of John Dobson,
architect, and Robert Grainger, builder, combined their talents
with those of others to create Eldon Square, Leazes Terrace,
Royal Arcade, Grey Street, the Theatre Royal, the Central
Exchange and Grey's Monument. Their achievements are
still visible today and Newcastle city boasts some of the finest
Georgian architecture and streets in the country.

In 1838 the city's oldest department store, Bainbridge's,
was formed. Soon afterwards Fenwick's store opened as did
Reid's the jewellers, all of which remain today. Places of
entertainment also grew in number with the building of the
New Tyne Theatre in 1867. Music halls flourished,
particularly the much-celebrated Wheatsheaf in the Cloth
Market where *The Blaydon Races* was sung for the first time
by Geordie Ridley. The vast, almost overnight transformation
of Newcastle into one of the nation's most economically
significant towns led to city status being awarded in 1882.
Surprisingly, popular opinion was against this change as it
was felt that something of Newcastle's spirit would be lost
in the process.

The striking new city of Newcastle entered the twentieth
century on a high note with a royal visit by King Edward VII
and Queen Alexandra in 1906. In his speech the king
commented: 'When we look around this great city we feel
that we are in one of the centres of industry which have raised
Great Britain to her present position in the hierarchy of
nations'. However, much of the optimism that was carried
over from the nineteenth century dispersed with the First
World War when a great deal of Tyneside men lost their lives
on French battlefields, whilst their women formed the
majority of the workforce in the factories back home.

In the period upon which this book focuses, the early to
mid-twentieth century, the economic background included
significant periods of slump and depression. Following the
First World War, Tyneside suffered extremely badly from a
fall in demand for munitions and ships. Famous hunger
marches ensued during this period of suffering and
depression. However, scratch beneath the surface and it is
also clear from the images in this book that life went on with
the same pinch of humour and optimism that it always had.
A lack of money was never sufficient to dampen the Geordie
spirit, and a strong sense of community prevailed right along
the banks of the Tyne. The resourceful nature of local people,
especially children, is also a feature of this book, along with
the determination of Geordies to succeed and enjoy life to
the fullest even during hard times.

The pictures and text that follow form a journey along one
of the nation's most important rivers – one that is held in the
utmost regard by its people. Throughout there is evidence
of the strong sense of community spirit and involvement
which makes Tyneside the unique, friendly and often quirky
area it is today, and seemingly always has been.

△ First records of Throckley show that it was originally part of the old manor of Newburn. The village is situated on the western boundary of Newcastle and was the home of George Stephenson, the great railway engineer, who spent his early years in the village at Dewley Burn. Throckley was synonymous with coal mining, an activity that had been a feature of the area since the thirteenth century (although it is recorded that the mines were abandoned in the seventeenth century and a new shaft was not sunk until the mid-eighteenth century). Throckley colliery was of major importance during the First World War. William Haswell Stephenson (see also page 44), mayor or lord mayor of Newcastle on seven occasions and famous as a philanthropist, was born in Throckley in 1836, as were his mother and father before him. The family lived at Throckley House and organised Sunday 'church' services in a small room on the upper floor of a local farmhouse. This marked the foundation of the Wesleyan Methodist Society the village. This view of Throckley village in the 1920s loc west along Hexham Road. The Wesleyan Church was buil 1871, with the church hall added in 1905, primarily for use a Sunday school. In the middle distance are the buttress walls of Throckley reservoir, currently the Henderson Filt water treatment works.

▽ Front Street in Throckley formed part of the old Newcas to Hexham road. At the left-hand edge of this view, dati from c.1910, is the former Throckley post office, with tobacconists next door followed by a confectioners and gene dealers. Adverts for Fry's chocolates and a sign for Lamb & Butler's Waverley Mixture tobacco can be seen in the sh windows. Dillons Fish Inn now occupies the post off premises whilst the remaining buildings are boarded up.

The Welfare Throckley 13366

Saturday half days and an early closing day for shops idweek increased leisure time for the 'masses' in the early ventieth century and encouraged the development of parks d recreational facilities. This picture of the Throckley Miners' elfare sports grounds, taken c.1930, shows the pavilion /hich contained changing facilities), tennis courts and >wling green. Bowls is an old-established sport but it was >t until the mid-nineteenth century that formal rules were troduced. Local and regional associations were subsequently rmed, one of the earliest being the Northumberland and urham Association in 1882. Tennis was particularly popular the early years of the last century since women could rticipate, which was unusual amongst major sports at the ne. Behind the pavilion is the football field where the rockley Welfare Football Club played their home games as embers of the North Eastern League.

Throckley tram terminus at Throckley crossroads c.1920.

Construction of Newcastle Corporation Tramways to the standard gauge commenced on 21 May 1878 with the operation of the lines being leased to Messrs Turton & Busby for the first 21 years. The first tram came into service on 23 December 1878. In 1914 the tramway was extended by three and a half miles westward from the old Scotswood terminus to Throckley Road Ends. In order to house tramcars that would serve the west of the city a new tram depot had been opened in Wingrove in 1904. Here tram No. 210 is emerging from Newburn Road en route to Heaton in the east of the city. St Mary's Church dates from 1887. The vicarage was added in the early twentieth century and was paid for by the congregation. Following the destruction of the Imperial cinema by fire on 12 December 1922, Throckley had been left without a cinema. However, on 15 May 1935 the Lyric cinema opened near Throckley crossroads on Newburn Road. It closed in 1966 to become a bingo hall before finally shutting in the mid-1970s when its owner was prevented from installing gaming machines.

△ These ten cottages were built in 1907 for elderly miners and were opened in June that year by John Bell Simpson. They are located on the north side of Hexham Road (the B6528) and were constructed under the auspices of the Northumberland Aged Mineworkers Homes Association (formed in April 1900) as a token of respect to the aged workmen of Throckley and Elswick collieries. The houses are still standing in excellent condition today.

▽ By the beginning of the nineteenth century a broad network of horse-drawn wooden-tracked railways had developed along the northern banks of the Tyne. These wagonways enabled horses to pull wagons containing coal and other goods between the collieries and the many coal staithes on the riverside (the staithes were designed to make loading coal into boats easier). The 'Dandy', seen here c.1906, consisted of a small-wheeled bogie attached to a rake of coal trucks. It wa used to carry firebricks from Throckley brickworks Lemington staithes. The route was on a steep gradient, so was no wonder that the horse preferred to travel in its wago on the downhill journey, during which the progress of th Dandy was controlled by brakes. George Stephenson, th railway pioneer, had recognised that controlling heavy loac on downhill gradients was particularly hard work for horse an observation that prompted him to say 'Let the horses ri downhill!'. Iron plate rails eventually replaced the timb tracks, enabling a horse to pull two loaded chaldron wagon rather than one. The last record of the Dandy operating Throckley dates from 1907, after which it was replaced by steam engine. This photograph was taken by Mr J. Green who sold it as a postcard from his shop in Throckley prior his emigration to Australia.

Throckley's memorial to the fallen of the First World War stands adjacent to St Mary's Church and vicarage. The main inscription reads 'In Honoured Memory of the men of Throckley who made the Supreme Sacrifice in the Great War'. Some 56 names are listed. In addition there is an inscription taken from John XV: 'Greater love hath no man than this, that a man lay down his life for his friends'. Here, men and women from Newburn and Throckley are gathered to pay their respects on Remembrance Day. The photograph was taken by Fred Hallam, a local photographer who lived in Throckley.

▽ Class B enclosed tramcar No. 309 was constructed by Brush and came into service in the mid-1920s – for a time it was run experimentally as a six-wheeled car. It was photographed at Throckley terminus on route 14. This was a revised route which ran from Heaton via Riverside, Central station and New Market Street, terminating at Throckley, and was one of the longest journeys that could be made on the network. The premises on the left belonged to T. Thomson Walker, carriers, who promoted themselves as providing 'For all road services'.

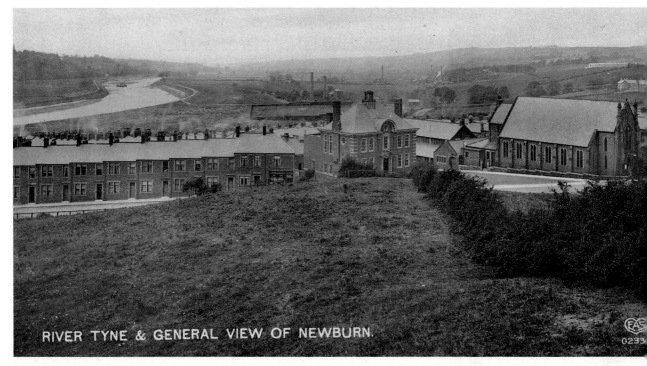

RIVER TYNE & GENERAL VIEW OF NEWBURN.

△ Newburn has Roman connections with Hadrian's Wall cutting across its northern half and continuing on through Throckley. The name derives from the New Burn which flowed through the old settlement into the Tyne. Newburn and nearby Lemington have always been amongst the greenest areas of Newcastle, and the majority of vegetables supplied to local markets in the eighteenth and nineteenth centuries came from here and Hexham. The urban district of Newburn was formed in 1893 and was integrated into the county of Tyne and Wear in 1974. Wylam lies to the west of Newburn, and it was here that George Stephenson, inventor of the railway, was born. He was married at Lemington Church and his remains are interred in the churchyard there.

The large building just to the right of centre in this c.19 picture was used as a dispensary and working men's clu Newburn Wesleyan Church, right, was built in the ear twentieth century, at which time some 4,000 people lived the area.

▽ Newburn seen from the eastern end of the High Stre c.1925. The tramway had been taken along the street in 19 as part of the extension of the line to Throckley. By this tim the area was no longer made up of small settlements farmers and fishermen, and a thriving community had grow up at Newburn with the expansion of the city ar improvements to transport links.

WORKING MENS' CLUB, NEWBURN.

Newburn Working Men's Institute comprised a library, [rea]ding rooms and lecture rooms which were used for [co]mmunity meetings. The working men's club movement [led] to a proliferation of such establishments all over the north [of] England as a result of growing industrialisation. They [pr]ovided a (hopefully sobering) alternative to the facilities of [vil]lage public houses. By 1925 the premises were being used [as] a dole office making subsistence payments to the local [un]employed. In 1990 they were adapted as a Social Services [re]sidential home for the elderly.

▽ Newburn in 1904 seen from the south bank of the Tyne looking north-east, with Newburn bridge prominent. In order to improve navigation on the river the Tyne Improvement Commissioners arranged for hand dredging and other works to be carried out in the late nineteenth century. This necessitated the building of a river crossing, and so Newburn toll bridge was built in 1893. In 1947 it was the last bridge on the Tyne to be freed of tolls.

△ Newburn toll bridge opened on Whit Monday in 1893, and this picture dates from about 40 years later. The northern platform of Newburn station is in the foreground. From 1748 the Wylam wagonway ran through Newburn to Lemington staithes using horse-drawn carts to transport coal from Wylam colliery to the staithes. The railway was subsequently upgraded to a 5 foot gauge iron track, and then converted to a standard gauge line in 1862. Part of the route was used by the Scotswood, Newburn & Wylam Railway. The line closed in 1968, but the wagonway can still be followed today as it is now a designated bridleway leading to the Tyne Riverside Country Park, developed in the 1980s. Newburn Hotel, situated at the corner of Grange Road and Station Road, was built in 1895 by F. M. Laing. It was a well-equipped hotel providing accommodation for commercial travellers and other visitors, along with stabling accommodation. In 1927 it was acquired by Robert Deuchar. Newburn bridge was fina[l] freed of tolls on 2 September 1947 when councillors fro[m] Northumberland and Durham Councils marked the occasi[on] by crossing the bridge.

▽ Removal vans such as this one would have been[a] relatively common sight in the suburbs of Newcastle duri[ng] the earlier decades of the twentieth century. They were main[ly] hired by colliery and shipyard owners and managers, as th[ey] were amongst the better-off in society and formed some [of] the very few owner-occupiers at this time. Alfred Bel[l's] headquarters were in the city centre at Higham Place. T[he] company regularly advertised its services in the local pre[ss] promoting the fact that it had 1,300, 1,000 and 600 cubic f[oot] vans in service, and would 'be pleased to quote for any loa[d] you may have for the Northern Counties'.

Grange Rd. Newburn-on-Tyne.

△ The expansion of large towns like Newcastle made city centre shops less convenient for day-to-day shopping, at least until the development of decent transport systems. Even then in poorer areas many families could not afford the tram fares for shopping trips. 'Corner' shops filled the gaps selling groceries, confectionery and everyday domestic necessities. This 1914 view, looking east towards Newburn bridge, features the hardware shop of G. Bullock, situated on Grange Road, which runs parallel to the Tyne.

▽ During the early part of the twentieth century the horse was used almost universally for transporting both people and goods via carts, buses and trams. It has been estimated that in the late Victorian period one horse was needed for every ten persons to keep society going. Here a horse waits quietly outside G. Bullock's shop in Grange Road, harnessed and ready to be loaded up with goods for his next delivery in the Newburn area.

Station Road and War Memorial, Newburn.

△ Looking up Station Road towards the Newburn war memorial *c*.1925. The Imperial Cinema (right foreground) was designed by Thomas Eltringham of Throckley colliery and opened on 18 October 1911, initially with 550 seats. A 131 seat gallery was added later. By 1919 it was doing such good business that two shows per night could not satisfy demand. During the inter-war years it was remembered as being a Spartan affair with a very cramped foyer, containing only a pay box and no confectionery kiosk. Following the opening of the Lyric Cinema at Throckley in 1935 the loyalty of its audience was divided. Nevertheless the owners carried out internal refurbishment and had a modern front elevation constructed. Despite these measures, it eventually became one of the many small cinemas to succumb to the impact of television, closing in 1961. It was used as a bingo hall for a short time afterwards and is now owned by Industrial Engravers, who produce signs, vehicle liveries and banners. Machetti's the confectioners, next door to the Imperial, were contracted by the cinema to supply sweets and ice-cream at the interval between the A and B films. The sign for Walter Willson, general dealer, can be seen at No. 7 Station Road.

◁ Newburn honoured its dead from the Great War by erecting this statue of a private infantryman in full kit. It was unveiled in 1920. Local families lost many men in the First World War, especially those who had joined the Northumberland Fusiliers, a local battalion that was decimated at the Somme in the first day of the battle, during which there were some 60,000 British casualties. This battle accounts for many of the names on the roll of honour on the statue.

In the 1860s it was recorded that Newburn had five ~~censed~~ premises, the Boat House Inn being one of them. The ~~i~~n lies alongside the Tyne on Water Row, almost opposite ~~th~~e Newburn Hotel. In the 1950s it was sold by the Duke of ~~N~~orthumberland to Newcastle Breweries who made ~~al~~terations and extensions to it. They disposed of it to private ~~ow~~ners in 1986. A number of dated flood marks on the outside ~~w~~alls demonstrate just how severely the level of the Tyne can ~~v~~ary. The river has always played an important role in the ~~lif~~e of the area, and in the 1840s an annual skiff race with a ~~£1~~00 purse was introduced; the route ran from the Tyne bridge ~~to~~ Lemington. The Boat House became the watering-hole for ~~m~~any thousands of spectators who descended on the riverside ~~to~~ watch what was billed as the 'Championship of the World'

and see some of the best-known names in competitive rowing during the nineteenth century. The first ever Tyne Regatta was held in 1834, and famous rowers like Harry Clasper, Robert Chambers and James Renforth were local heroes.

▽ W. Charlton and family photographed outside their home and the workshop of Mr Charlton's undertaking business in Newburn. In addition to undertaking, Mr Charlton advertised his services as a joiner, builder, cartwright, painter, glazer and paperhanger. It may have been in his capacity as cartwright that he came to be in possession of a cart belonging to the Throckley District Co-operative Society, but whatever the reason his daughter seems to be enjoying the opportunity to pose on it for a photograph.

△ There were several stages in the development of British cinema architecture and culture, one of which was represented by picturedromes, buildings which were renowned for their ornate plaster fronts and gaudy interiors. Here smartly turned out actors and actresses from the Newburn Picturedrome and Variety Palace have been photographed in Westmacott Street. They were out on the streets publicising their 'Grand Variety Program' which included The Gordon Girls, Ivy Dene, Llewllyn Hughes, The Gelders, The Goffs, Harry Morgan, Sisters Kenway and all! Why many of them have their middle finger raised is a mystery.

▽ The winding Newburn Road snakes its way downhill towards Newburn High Street with a tram ascending the single line incline to Throckley. In 1914 the publication *Tramways and Railway World* commented that 'The industrial undertakings up and down the River Tyne are numerous and most important, giving employment to multitudes of men, so that the tramway services constitute an essential feature in the life of the community'. Eventually, in 1946, buses replaced trams on the route to Throckley.

△ 'Football has been the overwhelming obsession of the north east working man throughout the twentieth century' (Harvey Taylor, *Geordies*, 1992). Almost every village and neighbourhood had a football team, and football formed the backbone of male North-East identity. Those that wanted to emulate their professional heroes but didn't have the talent still managed to play quality football for their local team. Here Newburn AFC line up for the photographer in the 1930s.

▽ The name of Spencer was closely identified with industrial progress in the North-East, and was also prominent in the world of philanthropy. John Spencer & Sons' steelworks extended across much of Newburn, the factory buildings spreading down the valley of the New Burn. The company

was a renowned manufacturer of steel and much of their output was sent down the Tyne to the shipyards for use in building liners, merchant ships and naval vessels. Indeed they produced plates for the liner *Mauretania*. Such was the influence of Spencer's that many of the streets in Newburn were named after its directors. Although the company was riding high in the early 1920s, it was not immune to the depression of the inter-war years and fell rapidly into decline during that period. £75,000 was needed to save the works, and the employees and public joined forces, placing adverts in local newspapers appealing for help. It was reported that workers were ready to invest part of their wages in the company, but despite this goodwill the works closed in 1926. The 130-foot chimneys were demolished in 1933.

The Village, Walbottle

◁ Walbottle is bounded to the west by Walbottle Dene, and to the east by Blucher. Originally Newburn and the surrounding area comprised many small scattered farmsteads, and in 1760 Walbottle came into the possession of the Duke of Northumberland (it had probably been a settlement since Saxon times). The green, seen here in 1929, lies at the heart of the village. It used to have a duck pond and a horse trough, and was widely used for recreational activities including maypole dancing and quoiting. A public air-raid shelter also temporarily occupied the green during the Second World War but was reputedly never used. The modern village of Walbottle was built in 1960.

◁ Most communities in England once had both a Primitive Methodist and Wesleyan chapel. This changed in 1932 after the Methodist Union which saw the two groups unite, although occasionally both chapels stayed open after the union. Walbottle had two chapels with the Wesleyan one, pictured here in 1915, eventually being designated Walbottle Methodist Church East.

Walbottle Farm.

◁ Agriculture had always been the main source of employment in Walbottle, there being some three farms within the village boundary. This view, dating from c.1914, shows Walbottle farm, which overlooks the north side of the village green. Walbottle remained a rural district for many years, and it was not until the twentieth century that it was absorbed into the extended boundaries of Newcastle. The development of factories and deep mines in and around the area provided employment opportunities for local people and as a result there was pressure to build housing on former agricultural land.

△ The Engine Inn in Walbottle is situated on the north side of Hexham Road (this view looks east towards Newcastle). Records suggest that it occupies the site of a stationary steam engine which had been used to haul wagons up the Walbottle incline to the northern collieries. The inn has had several name-changes over the years. In 1947 it was bought by Newcastle Breweries, later being renamed the Original Masons. It is currently called the Masons Arms. The substantial detached building in the distance is the Walbottle Co-operative store, a prominent landmark still standing today. It was recently occupied by Screenprint, but is currently vacant.

▽ Blucher looking west along the B6528 towards Walbottle, with the Co-op building in the far distance. The row of terraced houses on the left is Stephenson Terrace. The Vallum Roman wall passed between what later became the site of Simpson Terrace and the end of Stephenson Terrace. The Throckley Coal Company was responsible for building several streets of terraced houses in this area and they were all named after the directors of the company.

△ The growth of the coal industry in the early twentieth century contributed significantly to the development of Blucher. In 1800 a pit had been sunk in the vicinity and named after Field Marshall Blucher of Russia who, along with the Duke of Wellington, contributed to Bonaparte's defeat at Waterloo in 1815; this is where the village's name comes from. During the early nineteenth century a railway system at Blucher was the primary means of transporting coal down to the Tyne. Blucher colliery closed in the 1860s but was reopened in 1901 after being taken over by the Throckley Coal Company. It closed for good in 1956. West Spencer Terrace is one of a number of rows and rows of identical houses in Blucher. It runs in a line west from Spencer Terrace and lies between the old Hexham Road and the Coquet Buildings.

▽ All dressed up in their Sunday best, the younger generation stop to pose for a photograph on their way to Blucher Church in 1910. The boys are especially smart in their crisp white shirt collars, and some of the girls are wearing spotless white pinafores to protect their clothes. The mining community of Blucher was presented with its Methodist Chapel by Miss Kate Stephenson of the well-known Throckley family in 1906. The chapel was regarded as the centre of village culture, sport and politics. It is still standing today and acquired the organ from the Union Hall Road building when the latter closed.

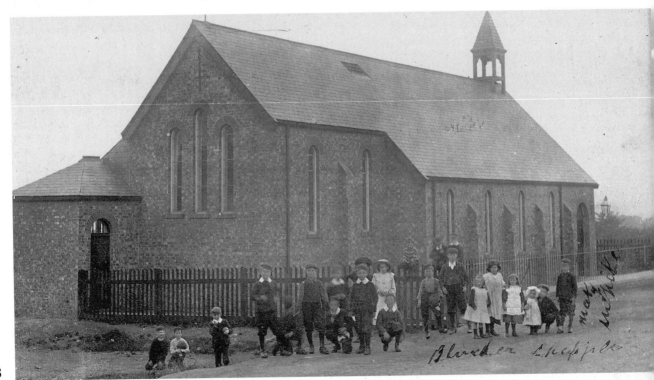

△ The name Lemington can be traced back to sixteenth century records which contain references to 'Lemandon staithes'. Coal was very important to the area, being transported to the Tyne at Lemington Point where it was carried by keelboats – small vessels that could navigate the shallower reaches of the Tyne – and delivered to collier brigs waiting below the old Tyne bridge. This photograph of Tyne View was taken from the corner of Northumberland Road c.1930. In 1931 the census confirmed there were 6,218 people living in Lemington. Between 1914 and 1922 the tram route through Lemington traversed two road bridges, the railway and then ran along Tyne View. Although the shops on the left are hidden by their awnings, the plumbing and ironmongers shop belonging to George Ellman Merrix at 1 Tyne View, and the confectionery shop of Misses Mary and Lena Garland at 6 Tyne View are prominent. The post office,

formerly run by postmistress Mrs Mason, is situated beyond the Garlands at No. 10. Lemington Hotel in Tyne View became the property of Scottish & Newcastle Breweries in 1959, but the licence was revoked in 1996.

▽ A Primitive Methodist Chapel was built in Tyne View in 1863, but the increasing size of the congregation called for the erection of a new chapel. This need was met by new premises which were built in Algernon Road to seat 320. The foundation stone was laid in May 1891 and the chapel opened in 1892. Various branches of Methodism united in 1932 and 40 years later, in 1972, Algernon Road and Union Hall Road Chapels merged to form the Lemington Methodist Church. The Robsons ran the family grocers and confectioners shop at 5 Algernon Road for a number of years. This photograph dates from c.1912.

Secondary Schools, Lemington. 8520

△ During the 1920s Lemington developed at a tremendous rate, and to accommodate this growth a secondary school was built. This postcard view was sent on 13 November 1927 by one of the teachers and the message reads 'we are having a most spiriting week of inspections'.

▽ At the end of World War I, less than two percent of all housing was owned by or rented from local authorities, and yet by 1973 47 percent of housing stock was owned by the city council. The bungalows belonging to private owner-occupiers at Dene Avenue were photographed in 1936. Dene Avenue runs north from the corner of Fernwood Road alongside the western verge of Sugley Dene.

Dene Avenue Showing Bungalows, Lemington. 8519

Sugley Villas, Lemington. 3740

△ Sugley Villas in Lemington, seen here in the early 1930s, lie just off Tyne View at its eastern end near Farnham Street. Newburn Hall School was situated in nearby Sugley Street.
▽ Seventeen miles of tram track were originally constructed in the city. Forty tramcars were used on the network with the cars hauled by a complement of 280 horses. However, by 1899 electrification of trams had commenced and another 21 miles of new line had been added, with the last horse tram running on 13 April 1901. By 1914 there were 63 miles of track with 211 electric tramcars. A single-line service from Scotswood bridge to Throckley started in 1914, and in this 1935 view tram No. 299 is seen heading towards the loop on the Lemington reserved track. This was the nearest access point for workers at the Lemington glassworks.

The Tyne ironworks was built on this site in 1797 an
produced a wide range of goods. It remained in busines
until 1886, after which the site was left to the elements. B
1906 the Newcastle & District Lighting Company had taker
part of it over, mainly for the manufacture of electric ligh
bulbs. Later, a power station, seen here in 1931, was buil
amongst the defunct ironworks buildings. One of th
partners in this enterprise was Sir Matthew White Ridley

Power Station Lemington

who also had considerable interests in coal and banking. The power station brought major environmental improvements to what was a highly polluted area. As well as providing power for the tramways, it was a source of electricity for local homes. Electricity represented a much cleaner source of energy than coal, and households gradually switched to the new power source.

△ The 1851 census produced the rather shocking statistic that only about 40 percent of the population regularly attended church. Nevertheless, quite apart from catering for the spiritual needs of their congregations, churches continued to play an important social role in society. They organised concerts and excursions, as well as providing meeting places and companionship. Here a group from Lemington Primitive Methodist C of E Society is seen at a social gathering dressed up to the nines in the year 1908. By 1914 records show that membership of the Methodist Church was beginning to decline.

▽ St Vincent's Orphanage was established in 1892 at the request of the Bishop of Hexham and Newcastle, and initially occupied premises in Brunel Terrace, off Westmorland Road. The children seen here in 1920 were under the care and guidance of the Sisters of Charity. In 1939 the orphanage accommodated children from what was then the Rescue Society, and during the Second World War its charges were evacuated to Chuseburn Grange, Dalton. The orphanage moved to premises on the West Road, near to Lemington Road End, in August 1950. However, in latter years there was not enough work to sustain the presence of the sisters and they withdrew from service in 1983. Despite this, the work of childcare still continues at this location, with preparation for fostering and the provision of accommodation for homeless young girls, mothers and babies.

△ Today this stretch of road through Denton is very busy with traffic, forming as it does one of the main routes into the city centre. The name Denton means 'the homestead in the field or valley'. This relatively quiet view from the early 1930s looks from the area commonly referred to as Denton Burn along the West Road, with Denton Bank still to be climbed in the distance. The area west of Newcastle was developed for housing from around the 1920s, and during that period the West Road was widened significantly from Wingrove westwards. The steep gradient at Denton Bank was eased by the removal of a chunk of the brow of the hill, just west of the Fox and Hounds pub. Denton post office, owned by the Law family, is to the left in this picture, while the adjacent advertising hoardings provide details of the forthcoming attractions at the Stoll Cinema (situated at the bottom of Westgate Road in the city centre) for the week commencing 7 August. The film being shown that week, *The Lost Chord*, starred John Stuart and Mary Glynne and was released in January 1933. Denton library now occupies the site on the right bounded by the white railings. It was opened on 19 July 1961 by Mr E. Popplewell, MP.

▽ Denton Burn photographed some ten years later, by which time trolleybuses were in operation in the area. These are evidenced by the overhead cables comprising pairs of parallel conductor wires (along which the trolley lead ran or slid) and the span wires, which were erected across the roadway, usually between poles. In October 1935 Newcastle Corporation introduced a trolleybus system which served the city well for over 30 years; by 1937 it had carried fifteen million passengers. Denton Burn services were extended another mile or so north to Denton Square and the turning circle at Copperas Lane. In 1937 the Denton Hotel was built at the north-east junction of West Road and Silver Lonnen Road by Arrol & Sons, brewers. Despite a lot of local opposition it was promoted as a modern hotel to cater for the growing popularity of the motorcar. It is still a flourishing public house today. Motor buses were licensed to run a service from Denton Burn to Cowen's Monument at the bottom of Westgate Road in 1934.

△ There was a steep wooded dene at Denton Burn running adjacent to Denton Road, and as it rolled down towards the Tyne it became a dumping area for vast amounts of rubbish. Denton became part of Newcastle upon Tyne under the Municipal Corporations Act of 1935. A motor bus service had been introduced from Denton Burn to Haymarket in June 1929, its route travelling along the West Road, then turning right down Denton Road and along the route that the trolleybuses would eventually take, to Whickham View and Pendower. It doubled back on itself to rejoin the West Road at the Fox and Hounds before travelling east along West Road to Westgate Road and on to the city centre. The confectioner's shop at 359 Denton Road was owned by the Vickery family and the butcher's shop next door at No. 357 belonged to Mr D. Douglas.

▽ The steep slope from Denton Road down to Scotswood Road near the junction of Fowberry Road (on the left). Mr E. S. Jameson's grocery store is also on the left, and further down the hill is the Blaydon & District Industrial and Provident Society Ltd.'s grocers (Scotswood branch). This view was published and sold as a postcard by Mr R. Walpole, who owned cash stores in nearby Scotswood Road.

△ Denton Road, this time viewed in 1906 from the junction with Prospect Terrace. Ingles' cash grocers shop was located at 1 Denton Road, but by 1908 the premises had been taken over by William Varty, who opened a fried fish dealers there. It remained a fish and chip shop for many years under the ownership of Mr J. Spoor before being acquired for use as a local sub-post office run by postmistress Mrs M. Henderson.

▽ This 1915 view of Chapel Terrace in Scotswood is taken from the junction of Prospect Terrace looking east towards Denton Road. Chapel Terrace was situated in the low Scotswood area towards the lower reaches of the Denton Burn and was demolished to allow for the widening of Denton Road. The building on the left is the United Methodist Chapel which could seat a congregation of 460. The properties beyond the chapel were shops. No. 7 was occupied by J. Steadman, beer retailer. The terrace also housed the Rose and Crown beer house, established in 1890 and comprising a shop, tap room, snug and cellar, plus a stable with three stalls in the yard. It was bought by Bass in 1920 for £2,000 but closed in 1923. The Alma Inn stood in this vicinity from the middle of the nineteenth century, and by 1896 had been reconstructed west of its original site. It closed in 1961 and was demolished in 1962.

△ Samuel Smith began trading as a tea merchant in Newcastle from a humble lock-up shop in Third Avenue in 1907, and thus Ringtons was established. The premises soon became too small for Smith's expanding business and he moved to an abandoned rifle range in Shields Road, Byker where the buildings provided the space urgently required. The horse-drawn cart seen here was a much admired sight on the streets of Newcastle, especially as it had a distinctive black, gold and green livery. Some of the teas on offer were Northumbrian blend, Green Label, Northern Pride, Valley View and the very progressive India African blend. On this occasion the delivery vehicle is on loan to Fenwick's, one of Newcastle's largest department stores, for the delivery of parcels.

▽ By 1926 the Ringtons tea company had opened a new head office in Algernon Road. A small number of motorised vans were in use by this period, one of which is pictured here along with two horse-drawn delivery vans, although the housewives of Tyneside much preferred to have their tea delivered by horse-drawn vehicle. It was not until 1954 that the mechanisation of the fleet was completed, although for sentimental reasons one horse van was kept on the road until the early sixties.

▷ Formed in 1883, Benwell Hill Cricket Club originally played on a ground situated on the present site of St Cuthbert's RC School in Benwell village, the approach being along the picturesque tree-lined Benwell Lane. The club joined the Tyneside Senior League in 1905 and the wooden pavilion in the distance of this picture was in place for the 1906 cricket season. This photograph shows the ground in 1911. Two years later, in 1913, the first eleven were champions. 1921 was a critical year for the club as the estate on which its ground was situated was sold and the club's tenancy terminated. A new ground was secured at Denton Bank that year, initially on a seven year lease, and the cricket team were again champions both in 1921 and 1922. The wooden clubhouse served the cricket community well until 1952 when a brick pavilion was built. Later a squash court was added and further extensions were made to the pavilion. The great English test player Tom Graveney was first introduced to the game at the original ground when he was six years old. At the time his father captained the Vickers Armstrong works side.

▽ The busy West Road as it appeared in the 1930s. Prior to the 1870s the west end of Newcastle was a commuting area for the middle and upper classes only, with the working classes traditionally housed in the slums and 'rookeries' in the city centre and on the steep northern slopes of the Tyne. Landowners in the west end waited until demand for their land was high before selling it, making enormous profits as private housing expanded in the area in the early 1930s. The building on the right is the Two Ball Lonnen Garage and the large structure beyond it is the Fox and Hounds public house, whose origins can be traced back to the beginning of the nineteenth century. For a long while it was owned by the Blackett Ord family and was a typical country inn before it was rebuilt in the early 1900s. It was bought by Deuchars in 1931 as residential properties began to rise all around it. The No. 2 double decker bus in the middle distance is heading for the city centre, a journey that took about 25 minutes from here.

△ Private housebuilding began to boom in the 1930s when incentives were introduced to encourage people to buy their homes. This was the start of the growth of owner-occupation, a trend which was halted temporarily by the Second World War. Owner-occupier estates began to appear at Denton and other suburbs in the west. A typical example of private housing from the period is Grange Road, seen here in 1935, which runs north from the West Road opposite Pendower Open Air School to Lonnen Avenue.

▽ The Embassy Cinema was planned as part of the new Thorntree housing estate at Denton Bank and designed by Robert Burke. There were plans for 626 stall seats and 362 circle seats, although only 936 seats were in place when the cinema was opened by the Lord Mayor of Newcastle, Alderman Grantham, on 6 October 1937. It was described at the time as having 'roomy, luxuriously upholstered tip up seats, ample free car parking and a futuristic scheme of decoration'. The opening film was *Pennies from Heaven* starring Bing Crosby. Using their best publicity shots, the cinema management advertised it as 'Newcastle's premier suburban cinema with a trolleybus to the door'. This view of the cinema and Ronald Drive was taken in 1938 when *Angel* starring Marlene Dietrich was showing. The Embassy, like so many other cinemas, suffered dwindling audiences as television grew ever more popular in the 1950s and was forced to close on 25 June 1960. It reopened as a bingo hall in 1963.

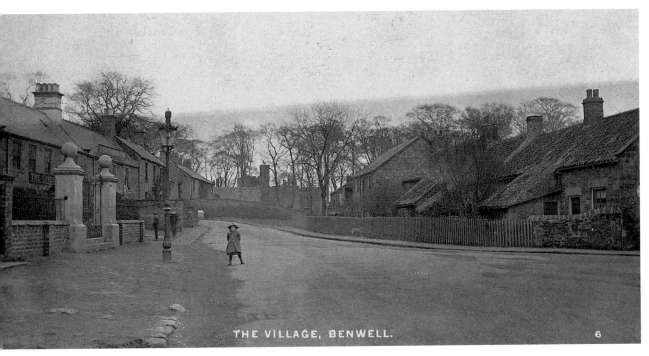

THE VILLAGE, BENWELL.   6

△ Benwell's recorded history stretches back to Roman times when Hadrian's Wall was built over Benwell Hill. There was a huge fort here, named Condercum by the Romans, and eventually a housing estate of that name was built here in the twentieth century. Benwell remained largely green until the early twentieth century. The population of industrial Tyneside expanded rapidly between 1850 and 1871 and large houses and estates were developed for local bankers and industrialists at Benwell from the 1880s onwards. This process peaked in 1900, and over time Benwell merged indistinguishably with Elswick. This was how the village looked in 1913.

▽ The premises of Samuel Boyd, at 73 Condercum Road, had been used as the Benwell Temperance Institute before being acquired for conversion to billiard rooms in 1912. Mr Boyd, the proprietor, is the formally-dressed gentleman seated in the middle of the photograph surrounded by a proud trophy-winning team. Billiards was played here until 1940 when the premises were taken over as a welfare centre.

Frith.   Robinson.   Hedley.   Rome.

Frazer.   Boyd.   Tait.

S. Boyd's Billiard Rooms, Benwell, 6 Tables.

▽ Smoke and grime pour out of the Charlotte pit, which was sited off Condercum Road in the early twentieth century. South Benwell, comprising 108 acres, was originally part of the larger Benwell Hall Estate. This land was purchased by John Buddle, a prominent mining engineer referred to as the 'king of the coal trade'. It was claimed he had a long-term speculative eye on the value of the land for housing development, but he initially acquired it for the underlying coal seams which were worked by himself and other colliery operators from the Paradise, Delaval and Charlotte pits. In 1887 the first streets adjoining Adelaide Terrace were built, essentially to attract pitmen from the nearby Charlotte colliery. This was operated by W. Cochran Carr who lived in South Benwell. It was eventually acquired by the Elswick Coal Company, who also owned the Elswick, North and South Benwell pits prior to nationalisation of the coal industry after the Second World War. The Charlotte pit closed in 1936.

▷ Windows full of general goods, produce and joints of mea are on view in this 1920s photograph of the shops belongin to F. Lawer the family butcher and W. H. Lawer, groce confectioner and tobacconist. The shops were located i Buddle Road, which links Atkinson Road to St John's Roa in the area of South Benwell. William Lawer was a shopkeep on Buddle Road from about 1909 to 1934, occupying premise at No. 263. In 1909 the shop next door at No. 261 was occupie by Miss Dolan, who traded as a confectioner, but by 1912 th premises were a butchers shop owned by J. Coffey. By 192 the Lawer family had expanded its empire and Frank Lawe was running the butchers shop (although by 1931 it ha changed hands again to the ownership of R. Davidson). Afte W. H. Lawer ceased trading as a grocer in 1934, the premise were taken over by Dalton Stores. No. 261 remained butchers until the late 1950s by which time the properties a 263 to 273 Buddle Road had been acquired by Hilda's Store

65. Benwell Parish Church, N C-on-Tyne.

△ Sunday school proved very successful in bringing together working class children for religious instruction. The processions they organised were originally religiou and temperate, bu by the end of the nineteenth century were becoming more social and ceremonial than spiritual. Here members of the Pride of Benwell Shepherds, juvenile branch, pose for a photograph aboar their attractive float following a procession in 1916 On such occasions each participating church would decorate one or two wooden frames and then fi them to flat carts normally belonging to a street trader. Ther was keen competition to see who had the best decorated cart.

△ The forerunner to the Benwell Parish Church of St James was a chapel of ease, but an increasing population led to the new church pictured here being built. Its foundation stone was laid on 4 July 1831 and the nave was completed a year later. Building work cost £1,668. The consecration ceremony took place on 8 October 1832 and was conducted by Bishop Grey of Bristol. In 1864 an aisle was added, and an organ chamber constructed in 1879. This 1909 photograph shows the completed church, which had developed into a passably handsome building after the tower was raised in 1894 and a peal of bells and clock added.

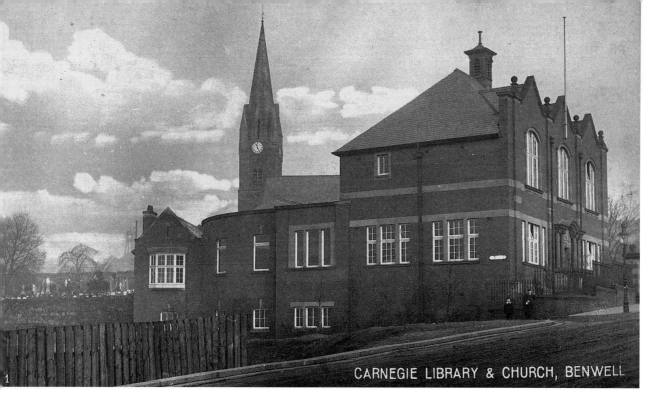

CARNEGIE LIBRARY & CHURCH, BENWELL

Alderman Newton, chairman of Newcastle Corporation public libraries committee, informed committee members in the early 1900s that 'a large population had sprung up in Benwell and in such a densely populated district the chief necessity was to provide some intellectual culture'. The Carnegie branch library, funded by Mrs Carnegie (widow of the great Scottish industrialist and benefactor Andrew Carnegie), was built in 1908 for the sum of £5,000, the contractor being Jacob Parkinson & Son. It was only the fourth branch library to be built in the city.

In the second half of the nineteenth century Sunday schools played an important role in promoting literacy and basic education, as well as providing religious instruction to children and young people. The movement also organised social activities in the form of festivals, parades and choirs. The majority of working class children attended Sunday school where they could experience the colour and excitement provided by choral concerts, street processions and trips. Here members of the Boundary Street Mission Band of Hope and Benwell Presbyterian Church Sunday school are well wrapped up in hats and scarves on what must have been a rather cold day, especially for handling their various gaily coloured but heavy banners. The Band of Hope's temperance institute was located at 148 Westgate Road, but this photograph was taken outside Benwell Presbyterian Church.

△ At the end of the First World War less than two percent of all housing was owned by or rented from local authorities. The overwhelming majority of working class housing belonged to private landlords, who owned 90 percent of all homes. Prior to 1919 only 622 council houses had been built in Newcastle, yet from 1925 to 1939 an average of 774 a year were constructed. In 1919 the Addison Act empowered local authorities to provide working class housing assisted by a state subsidy. The Pendower estate in west Newcastle was Benwell's first housing estate and demonstrated the generous application of the Act, which set rent independently of costs. The new developments tended to be cottage-type estates of single or semi-detached family dwellings with small front gardens, designed by private architects. Pendower Way runs downhill from Fox and Hounds Lane to Benwell Lane, and here the local coalman poses proudly beside his horse and cart before continuing on his rounds of the area.

▽ Happy, glum, anxious, wary and unsure expressions are evident on the faces of these children as the new intake of pupils at Pendower Open Air School ponder what lies ahead of them on the day of their arrival, 1 October 1925. The school faced the West Road in the 'Condercum' area of the city. Its classrooms only had fixed walls on their northern sides, with partitions to the other three sides designed to allow vast amounts of fresh air into what became 'outdoor' classrooms in the summertime. The children who attended suffered from a range of ailments, and sunshine, rest and exercise were the dominant factors in aiding their recovery. The school building is still in use today as an educational development centre.

The establishment of the Post Office Savings Bank in September 1861 was a key date in the development of post offices in the UK. It was the first measure that marked a move away from post offices being solely linked to the Royal Mail. Within two years there were 2,500 post offices nationally, rising to 8,000 by the mid-1880s, handling 3.5 million accounts. In 1909, about the time of this photograph of West Benwell post office, a service for the handling and distribution of old-age pensions was introduced. The issue of car licences followed and during the First World War years the post office was instrumental in floating a war loan scheme. West Benwell post office, commonly referred to as the 'post and money office', was an integral part of a general dealers' undertaking situated at 4 Oliver Street (formerly Tyne Street), and was owned by the Carr family for a few years before the First World War.

▽ The Adelaide Hotel was built in 1903 on the corner of Elm Street and Adelaide Terrace. This rare photograph of an Edwardian public house interior shows the landlord behind the bar with his staff (landlords were highly-regarded figures in working class society). In 1908 there were 100,000 pubs in England and Wales and the handsome fixtures and fittings of the Adelaide Hotel must have been a welcome sight for local people who lived in poor housing and cramped conditions. Runners from the Elswick Harriers were regularly to be seen passing the pub on their training route from Benwell Church through the west end suburbs and on to Bentinck Road.

Elswick Rd. N C on Tyne.   (136)

△ The earliest westward expansion of Newcastle city took place in Elswick. A vast tract of land sloped steeply down to the Tyne at Scotswood and after it was publicly announced in 1883 that a 'new town' was planned, work commenced in 1884. The area along Elswick Road (pictured here) and Westmorland Road began to be developed for housing and shopping, and in 1877 the first residential streets were built adjoining Adelaide Terrace. By 1891 nearly half the population of the city lived in Elswick and Westgate, and by 1903 Benwell and Elswick had run into each other. Lord Armstrong built many of the rows of terraced houses that were constructed in Elswick to house workers from the shipyards and engineering works on the Tyne, and the district became densely populated by the working classes. Many streets were named after the directors of Armstrong's factory.

The first headquarters of Elswick Harriers were located i Elswick Road in the Chesterfield Arms public house.

▽ Looking west along Elswick Road around 1930, with group of schoolchildren on the left carrying their tenni racquets in readiness for a game at nearby Elswick Park. Th imposing building on the right is the John Knox Presbyteria Church, which was situated on the corner of Beech Grov Road until its demolition in the 1950s. It was designed t seat a congregation of 800 and had spacious cloakrooms fo the greater comfort and convenience of worshippers. Th laying of the foundation stone took place on 29 Novembe 1895, the ceremony being performed by Sir George Barcla Bruce. There had been a pressing need for this new church a the old sanctuary in West Clayton Street was too cramped.

John Knox Church, Elswick Road, Newcastle.   4838

During the 1880s the Amateur Athletics Association became the dominant force in athletics. Elswick Harriers were founded in 1889 under the auspices of 'true amateur athletics' and soon developed into a well-organised and popular running club in the west end of the city. Pictured here is the Elswick northern team that lined up for the Northern Counties junior cross-country championships at Haydock Park, Manchester on 15 February 1908. Many of the athletes worked in the local mines, steel foundries and heavy engineering works. Thirty-eight clubs participated and Frank Melville (No. 367 in the picture) won the race. He had also won the Morpeth to Newcastle road race earlier in the year and went on to become Elswick's first international runner, representing England.

It is worth noting that until as late as the 1920s some 80 percent of retail sales were made in independent shops rather than chain stores. People used local independent shops for a number of reasons. Many were open all hours and local grocers would offer a personal service and could meet particular requests for goods. Most importantly of all many gave credit to trusted customers, thus easing the wait for pay day, and it was measures such as these that allowed small traders to hold on to their customers in the face of increasing competition. E. Wilkinson first began trading with a cash grocers' business (i.e. one that did not offer credit) at 10 Mill Lane as early as 1888, and by 1895 had acquired further premises at 2 Ravensworth View (off Elswick Road). He lived at 32 Adelaide Terrace, New Benwell, about half a mile from his first shop. The Ravensworth View premises were shared between two businesses, and at different stages Mr Wilkinson's fellow occupants included a bootmakers, fruiterers and confectioners. By 1906, the date of this view, J. Jones 'The Noted Bacon Shop' occupied the premises. The grocery business closed in the early 1900s although the bacon shop appears to have survived until the First World War.

◁ The 1920s saw the expansion of the west end allowing retailers to grow and flourish as ever-increasing numbers of potential customers moved to the area. The growing factory production of everyday commodities made it possible for those with little or no experience of the retail trade to set themselves up as self-employed shopkeepers at very little cost. John Brown took over the confectioners business of J. Clark at 252 Mill Lane in 1904 (the lane leads from Elswick Road north to Westgate Road). Records show he was in business for ten years or so before the premises transferred to D. Scott around 1914. His profession was that of a craneman.

▽ Horse-drawn vans such as this one were a familiar sight on the streets of Newcastle in the early 1900s. This particular example collected washing from homes, took it to the laundry for cleaning and then returned it to its owner. It was photographed c.1908 and belonged to the Woodbine Laundry, Elswick Road, who also advertised a 'carpet dusting' service. The laundry was established in 1902 and existed for over 70 years. By the time of the First World War horse-drawn vans were gradually being replaced, giving way to motorised transport. The laundry had plenty of work as Elswick expanded from a population of 3,500 to a massive 59,000 in the 50 year period from 1851 to 1901.

▷ When this photograph was taken during the First World War, Newcastle's major factories were concentrated along the riverside, and the great bulk of tram traffic had to be carried on the one main route running parallel to the Tyne. Scotswood Road, off which the extensive Elswick Works was situated, groaned under the succession of peak hour tramcars. (Nearly 200 tramcars were carrying more than 45 million passengers a year on the system at the time.) In May 1915, as a wartime measure, fourteen women were trained as tram conductors by Newcastle Corporation Tramways. They were paid three shillings an hour during the training period, a sum that was reduced to sixpence an hour when they started work on the trams. The rope being held by the female tram conductor in this picture was used to swing the pole on top around when the tram reached its terminus and before it began its return journey. Part of the message on the reverse reads 'How do you like our lady tram conductors. Don't you think they are smart.'

◁ Tramway employees enjoyed secure work, a free uniform and paid holidays. Here, tram conductor No. 1134 poses with the tools of his trade. As well as being used to punch tickets on trams, bell punches such as the one attached to the strap of the conductor's satchel were used by trolleybus conductors until 1948. The satchel was used to keep cash in from the purchase of tickets, and the box under his arm stored unused tickets for sale. Different coloured tickets were used for varying stages on the route. Councillor Mayne was vice-chairman of the Newcastle Corporation Tramways committee in 1914 and remembered seeing a passenger carrying a large washing tub onto a tram, taking it on a journey of nearly two miles for his fare of a penny. The conductor suggested he should bring the mangle with him too on the next trip.

▷ William George Armstrong was born in Shieldfield and initially trained as a solicitor. However, he had a talent for engineering and in 1847 bought a five acre site at Elswick in order to build a new engineering works. At the outset it employed 180 men, producing hydraulic cranes and later a range of armaments. A rifle-barrelled breach-loading field gun built for the British army at the time of the Crimean War was recognised

Site of Lord Armstrong's Works in 1856.
(From an old Calotype Paper Negative)

as the finest of its kind in the world. Armstrong was destined to become the greatest northern English Victorian of his time. The building of the Swing bridge on the Tyne in 1876 and works by the Tyne Improvement Commissioners to widen the river and improve navigation paved the way for ships to reach the Elswick river front, thus allowing Armstrong's works to expand. This picture shows the site of his original works.

▽ In 1882 Armstrong's merged with Mitchell & Co. (who had a yard in Walker) to build warships at the former's Elswick yard. The company was involved in another merger in 1897, this time with Whitworth's of Manchester, giving rise

to Messrs Armstrong, Whitworth & Co. William Armstrong also acquired the Scotswood Shipbuilding Company and at their peak his combined Tyneside works were the largest industrial concern in Europe, employing over 20,000 people and spanning a vast 230 acres. Improvements to the Tyne included the establishment of better loading points for coal and goods, which benefited riverside industrial concerns such as Armstrong's. By 1925 there were six major coal loading points on the river, including Dunston staithes and West Dunston staithes which were owned by the London & North Eastern Railway. A considerable number of smaller staithes including Elswick, made a significant contribution to loading facilities and ensured a quick turnaround of trade.

▷ The assembly line in full swing inside Armstrong's Elswick works with the construction of light tanks underway. During the inter-war years the fall in demand for munitions and ships forced another merger on Armstrong's, and a partnership with Vickers came about in 1927. In order to try and buck the downward trend in business, the company subsequently embarked on a policy of reorientation, producing for example railway engines for the Empire while continuing to supply the British army with armoured machine-gun carriers. Shipbuilding and heavy engineering were amongst those industries hardest hit by the inter-war depression and the decline left thousands out of work. Because of its strategic importance to the war effort, the Germans subjected the Elswick works to several air raids in 1940.

▽ At 11.00 p.m. on Tuesday 14 September 1909 a goods train accidentally got onto a private railway line belonging to Armstrong, Whitworth & Co. at Elswick which ran parallel to the GNER's Carlisle line. It crashed into one of the firm's locomotives, which was stationary. Four crewmen were injured. Three of these were from Leeds, while the fourth, Robert Martin Shillady, who had the job of navigator, was from Gateshead. The newspaper account at the time said that 'Shillady was too ill to explain how the tragedy occurred'. Elswick fire brigade had been immediately informed of the tragedy as the derailment brought down a telegraph pole, creating the danger of fire. All four men were rushed to the Royal Infirmary suffering from injuries including scalding. The next day two of them were well enough to return home to Leeds, but Shillady was less fortunate and later died. The result of an enquiry into his death concluded that the accident was due to a misconception on his part that the train was on the main line and not an independent line. It should have stopped at the long distance danger signal, at which point signalman John Blaylock would have set the points to the main line. However, Shillady drove past the signal at 25 miles an hour and the signalman's efforts to stop the train by the use of red lamps and a whistle proved unsuccessful.

△ During the Victorian era parks became a high civic priority, providing as they did opportunities for fresh air and exercise. In the late nineteenth century, William Haswell Stephenson was one of a syndicate of six who bought the land on which Elswick Park now lies. It had been offered for sale as building land, but the syndicate acquired it so that it could be kept intact until Newcastle Corporation took it over as a public park. Stephenson also presented the city with its first branch library, which was built on the edge of the park. Elswick Park (originally named West End Park), lies between Elswick Road and Westmorland Road and dates from 1878, making it one of the first parks to be established in Newcastle. The imposing building in the background is Elswick Hall, which stood in the middle of the park. Designed by William Stokoe in 1803 it was the one-time residence of Richard Grainger, and had its own stables and servants' quarters. Having fallen into a state of disrepair, plans were mooted to demolish the hall and build an adventure playground on its site. These were not followed through, although the building was eventually pulled down anyway and the Elswick Park Leisure Pool, opened on 20 January 1981, now occupies its site.

▽ In the late nineteenth century Newcastle had more open spaces reserved for public recreation than any other city in the country. Parks were usually places of great pleasure, well-maintained and immaculately set out, and Elswick Park was a peaceful rural escape in the middle of the booming conurbation. Like so many of Newcastle's parks, Elswick was also an important social arena – a place to court, stroll with friends or have fun with the family. Men played pavement draughts using poles to move their pieces over the marked squares, while in 1909, when this photograph was taken, the lake was a major attraction, especially for children who fished for tiddlers or sailed toy boats. The park originally had a bandstand but part of the swimming pool complex now occupies its site.

△ The first trolleybus route opened in 1935 following a decision a year earlier by the city council to replace the trams. By 1940 113 trolleybuses were operating six services in the city. The trolleybus in this view was brought into service on 1 October 1950 and is en route to Denton Road terminus via Elswick Road. The fleet was painted cadmium yellow with cream roofs and window surrounds. In the 1950s 200 trolleybuses were operating in the city, but at this period the role of the motorbus was expanding with 250 in service by then. Trolleybuses lacked the ability to manoeuvre, were route-bound and not able to overtake. Also, their average speed compared unfavourably with motorbuses. This particular trolleybus was withdrawn from service in 1966 and disposed of to Autospares (breakers) of Bingley.

▽ Public parks evolved out of a Victorian concern that – in overcrowded urban areas – lack of open space was a major factor behind increases in crime and drinking among the poorer classes. Medical opinion also held that infectious diseases were transmitted through pollution in the air, and that urban parks would help check this. In 1834 a Select Committee on Drunkenness recommended 'the establishment of . . . gardens or open spaces for athletic and healthy exercises in the open air'. Cruddas Park is bounded by George's Road, Scotswood Road and Brunel Terrace with the former St Vincent's Orphanage sited on its northern boundary. It offered much-needed open space in a neighbourhood of dense housing. However, while one group advocated parks, they were seen by some as being an inducement to absenteeism as they were more attractive than going down the pit or working at the factory! The swings on the left have the words 'For Boys Only' painted on the crossbar.

St. Anne's Convent of Mercy, Newcastle-on-Tyne.

△ The nuns of the St Anne's Convent of Mercy enjoy some quiet pastoral time in this 1910 view of their grounds. The convent had been located on this substantial site off Elswick Road since the late nineteenth century. When the building changed use in 1954 to become a Catholic school, several of the teachers found themselves drawn closer to the church and went on to take their vows as nuns. The school gave 30 years of educational service before being converted to a Marie Curie hospice.

▽ The order of the Little Sisters of the Poor began life in 1866 based at premises in Clayton Street in Newcastle city centre, where 40 elderly residents were housed. It later moved to the much bigger St Joseph's Home in Westmorland Street (illustrated here), and by 1966 provided shelter to 200 residents. The home was described as 'a large cultivated oasis in the centre of a crumbling Elswick' and was regarded as half hotel and half hospital. Qualification for residency remained constant throughout the order's lifetime: 'over sixty and poor'!

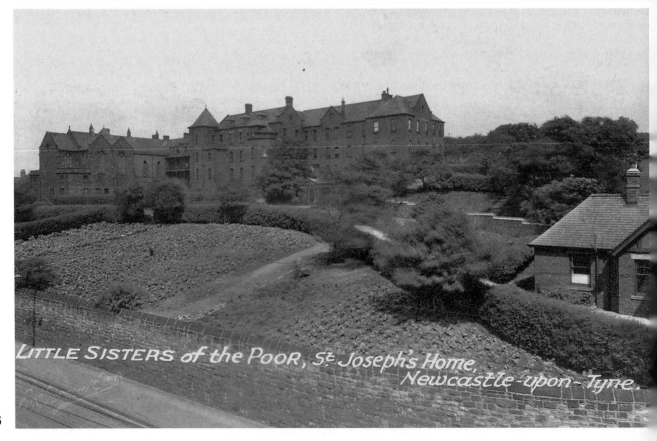

LITTLE SISTERS of the POOR, St Joseph's Home, Newcastle-upon-Tyne.

Scotswood Road runs west from the cattle market and closely follows the banks of the Tyne to Scotswood bridge. In its heyday it was generally considered to be a most pleasant place for ladies to shop: lit by tilley lamps, the shops often stayed open well into the evening with many goods prominently displayed on the pavements. A whole range of shopping could be done on Scotswood Road with its fruiterers, butchers, bakers and newsagents, while the store of Todd Brothers at Nos. 176–184 (on the right in this view) was almost the size of a small department store. The Maid of Derwent Inn was located at No. 174, and beyond Todd Brothers, at No. 186, was the Empire Confectionery Company.

In the 1930s it was recorded that there was a licensed premises every 80 yards on Scotswood Road. None of these buildings remain on Scotswood Road today.

▽ In 1910 some 12,000 amateur football clubs were registered with the Football Association. Factories, youth clubs, churches and schools across the UK turned out teams who played regularly in a variety of local leagues. Scotswood AFC are featured on this postcard from 1915, the year in which they were winners of the Northumberland Aged Miners Cup. The card was sent by someone living at 32 Shafto Street, Scotswood.

△ Designed by architect John Green of Newcastle and built at a cost of £15,000, the Scotswood suspension bridge was completed on 16 April 1831. It was reported that 20,000 people crossed over the bridge to Blaydon on the opposite side of the Tyne that day to commemorate the opening, although first to cross was the Lord Mayor and his entourage. The bridge served Tyneside for over 130 years before being demolished and replaced in 1967 by a modern structure.

▽ In 1914 most of Newcastle's residents were within five minutes walk of a tramway. During the morning peak 100 special tramcars were run for workmen. The great factories lay near the Tyne at the extreme eastern and western boundaries of the city, and 12,000 workers enjoyed special fares. The penalty for this was that the trams were bursting at the seams. Here a tramcar is entering the turning loop at Scotswood bridge. Before doors were fitted, riding on the top deck was like sitting in a wind tunnel as the draft came up the front stairway and went down the rear one! Many trams in the region carried the legend 'Shop at Binns', an advertising campaign that was down to William Naples, a draper. He had joined Binns in 1918 when it was a small shop in Sunderland. After becoming general manager he negotiated a contract with Sunderland Corporation in 1921 to carry the advertisement on their trams at a price of £1 a year per car. Similar deals were secured with other North-East transport operators.

△ Shafto Street, photographed here on 15 August 1917, is situated at the far western end of Scotswood Road, not far from the site of Chapel Terrace (see page 27). It links Whitfield Road to Armstrong Road. Records show that tradesmen mainly resided in the street with occupations represented including wheelwrights, joiners, blacksmiths, tailors and engine drivers at the time this photograph was taken.

▽ In 1902 H. Barnfather, clock and watchmaker, was based at 317 Scotswood Road and advertised himself as a 'practical watchmaker'. Here the shop window is full of lines of superb pocket watches, which was appropriate since early twentieth century society was very time-orientated and people placed great store by having the correct time.

◁ This picture postcard has a note on the reverse revealing that it shows the 'new Scotswood Church', photographed in 1916. It is likely that the well-dressed gentlemen are representing the firm of architects, Messrs Hicks & Charlewood of Newcastle, and the contractor, Mr S. F. Davidson of Newcastle who, together with a church representative, are probably carrying out an inspection of building progress to date. When completed this became the Scotswood Parish Church of St Margaret, situated on Armstrong Road at the junction of Heighley Street, opposite the site of the former Denton Road Infants' School and next to Scotswood library (now the Scotswood Family Learning Centre).

▷ St Margaret's Church was built between 1915 and 1917. It was constructed of stone in the style that prevailed at the end of the fourteenth century and measured 126 feet long. The building comprised a nave and chancel with north and south aisles, baptistery, organ chamber, clergy and choir vestries. Here a group of painters with their Castle brand tins of paint prepare to apply the finishing touches. When constructed the church had no tower, just a fleche, a slender wooden spire at the centre of the roof. Dr Straton laid the foundation stone on Saturday 24 July 1915 in what was virtually his last act as Bishop of Newcastle. The building was consecrated in 1917, marking the climax of the work of the Church at Scotswood and the realisation of a dream for the congregation of 600. Funds had been raised from public subscriptions, aided by a grant from the Fenwick Legacy Fund.

St Margaret's Church & Bridge Crescent, Scotswood.

△ The corrugated iron forerunner to the stone St Margaret's Church can be seen in the foreground of this view of Bridge Crescent, Scotswood, looking towards part of the vast Armstrong factory. Records suggest that work on the church may have commenced during the incumbency of the Revd Wm. Maughan, the first vicar of Benwell. Church day schools were opened in April 1870 but services were not held in the village until 1885. The first church, seen here, was not built until 1895 and was known locally as the 'Iron Building'. It served the community well as a temporary place of worship until the new St Margaret's was built. As the congregation fell in number over time the corrugated iron church had to be sold. It was used variously as a Labour Exchange and Scout Headquarters before being turned into the Regent Cinema in 1926. This operated successfully into the 1950s, but closed on 6 July 1957 'owing to lack of business'. After that the building became a bingo hall and music club before finally being demolished in February 1964 to make way for the approach roads to the new Scotswood bridge.

▽ At the beginning of the twentieth century the early morning round of the dairyman with his pony and trap carrying churns of fresh milk was a familiar sight on the streets of Newcastle. Mr J. J. Armstrong plied his trade as a milkman in the Scotswood area during the 1920s. Milk used to be dispensed to housewives into jugs by tapping or ladling it from the churns. In 1921 Newcastle City Council appointed inspectors tasked with taking steps to improve milk distribution. It was their job to ensure that more hygienic methods of milking and delivering milk were developed.

△ Bridge Crescent connected Prospect Terrace and Scotswood Road. Corner shops were the focal point of all communities, literally because of their position, and if the corner site wasn't occupied by a shop there was usually a pub there instead! T. Anderson & Sons had their grocers and fruiterers shop in Bridge Crescent for the majority of the inter-war years. This was a very busy thoroughfare so the boys with their hoops and sticks, one of the favourite toys of the day, would have had to be wary and keep the hoops under control. The well-known clock tower of the Ord Arms is prominent at the end of the terrace. The 1950s and 1960s was the era of the bulldozer and at that time much of the west end of the city was classed as 'unfit for human habitation'. Early areas to be cleared were at the city end of Scotswood Road and included all the buildings illustrated here.

▽ Situated only a few yards from Scotswood railway station,

the Ord Arms stood on the corner of Bridge Crescent. The original pub was a small building named after the Ord family of Fenham Hall and occupied the same site as the magnificent and imposing building seen in this 1908 view. The new building, with its splendid clock tower, dated from the beginning of the twentieth century, the proprietor at the time being Mr R. W. Metcalf. The Ord family, later the Blackett-Ords, had extensive holdings of land to the west and north of Benwell. Until the 1870s the pub had its own brewery house and when it was auctioned in 1898 it comprised a bar, parlour, snug, newsroom, billiards and club room, and also had three bedrooms. It was bought by the Laing family and rebuilt in 1900. In 1937 the Ord Arms was purchased by Robert Deuchar, passing into the ownership of Newcastle Breweries in the 1950s. Although demolished many years ago, the pub's clock tower was salvaged, carefully dismantled, and re-erected at the headquarters of the Scottish & Newcastle Brewery in the city.

The Denton Burn ran between the western boundary of Blackett Terrace and the back of Ridley Terrace. Blackett Terrace, the northern end of which adjoined Scotswood Park, disappeared in the 1970s when Denton Road was widened.

Scotswood bridge was first opened in 1831 when it, and the adjoining road from the old boundary of the City of Newcastle, was the property of a company that levied a toll. Here a pedestrian can be seen handing over his one penny to the toll-keeper to cross the bridge. Great efforts had been made for many years to have the toll abolished, but it was only removed as a result of the bridge being taken over by Newcastle Corporation at a cost of £36,300. This occurred when Benwell was incorporated into the city. The ceremony marking the abolition of tolls took place on 18 March 1907, not long after this postcard was produced. Councillor Johnstone Wallace declared the bridge free at a gathering attended by members of Newcastle City Council, plus representatives of Durham Council and Gateshead Corporation. The councillor's horse-drawn carriage was the first vehicle to cross the bridge for free, followed by a motor cavalcade and large numbers of pedestrians. Local residents came out in force to experience crossing and re-crossing the bridge without charge. The first free journey was made thirty minutes after the announcement of the abolition tolls, but unfortunately nobody seemingly informed the staff of the Blaydon tollgate on the south side of the river. They still demanded and received the normal toll for a short while.

△ Built in 1835 to provide easier communication between Collingwood Street and the cattle market on Scotswood Road, Neville Street takes its name from Neville Tower, which formed part of the original town wall. The Neville family whom the tower was named after lived at Raby Castle in County Durham. The building on the right, with its fine colonnade and portico, is the Central railway station, which was designed by John Dobson and built between 1846 and 1850, although his plans for the portico were rejected. Neville Street was widened in 1847 to make way for Central station and the opening of the Newcastle & Berwick Railway. A portico designed by Thomas Prosser, the North Eastern Railway Company's own architect, was finally added in 1863. A stream of trams can be seen in service in this 1911 photograph.

▽ The old Castle Keep and Black Gate photographed in 191 After the Norman Conquest, a fortified site at Newcast became a strategic imperative in order to control the rive crossing and the location's possibilities as a port. In 1080 Rober son of William I, had a wooden fort built – this was called 'New Castle'. The surviving keep dates from 1172–77, with the Blac Gate dating from 1247. The town walls were added in th thirteenth and fourteenth centuries, while the flag tower an battlements visible in the picture date from the nineteent century. Some of the interior fittings in the great hall of th keep came from the old Beehive Inn located on Sandhill. Th railway line into Central station was built through the heart o the castle site, dividing the keep and Black Gate. It is doubtfu whether such a ruthless commercial decision would be allowe to impinge upon such an important antiquity today.

The High Level bridge connecting Newcastle and Gateshead was designed by Robert Stephenson and Thomas Elliot Harrison. Able to carry railway traffic on its upper deck and road vehicles on the lower one, it was opened by Queen Victoria in 1849. A couple of years before this photograph of 1924 was taken, the High Level bridge had been strengthened to enable it to carry electric trams on the lower deck, and by 1923 services had been introduced across the Tyne. A horse-drawn service had been operational from the 1880s and lasted for 50 years, finally being withdrawn in 1931, despite repeated allegations of cruelty to the horses. A brake, jointly operated by T. Howe and Works Contractors Ltd., is approaching the bridge in this picture. The brakes carried up to 40 passengers and the fare was half a penny. As the firm only had to pay a 4d toll, the enterprise was hugely profitable.

▽ The 'lady window cleaners' were a familiar sight in and around Newcastle, especially during the war years when women undertook the traditional work of men who were away fighting in foreign lands. The City & Suburban Window Cleaning Company, who had their head offices at 50 Grainger Street, employed the cleaners.

The lady window cleaners of Newcastle.

◁ Postal deliveries by women came to prominence during World War I as men left to join the forces and women took over their duties. It wasn't until 1872 that all of the country's postal delivery staff started to wear uniforms, and during the First World War postwomen wore navy blue serge tunics and blue straw hats. The hats remained in service until 1929 when a more fashionable felt hat, in the style of that worn by the Girl Guides, was introduced. This particular postwoman, photographed in 1917, is dressed in unofficial garb comprising a jacket and non-regulation hat. It is possible that she was an early volunteer. Collection times were changed during the war years and the notice on the pillar box would have advised the public of the revised service.

▽ Vegetarianism is generally thought of as a modern phenomenon, borne out of increased health awareness and dietary concerns. Thus the sight of a vegetarian cafe in Newcastle in the early years of the twentieth century is somewhat surprising. The Market Vegetarian Cafe, advertised here on a

postcard shortly after it opened in 1906, was situated at 4 Cloth Market and had another branch at 4 Nelson Street. Originally an ironmongers, the Cloth Market site's new occupiers offered 'tasty nutritious dinners at moderate prices' and boasted of their 'famous sixpenny teas'. The venture appears to have been unsuccessful, however, as by the beginning of the First World War the premises had been vacated and were not occupied again until 1918 when J. Pembrey, booksellers, took them over. Later the building was used by Humble & Glenton, a firm of chartered accountants. By the 1950s it was the home of the northern branch of the National Union of Tailors and Garment Workers, and it is still in use today as a trade union centre.

Captioned 'Street urchins', this postcard view of children playing barefoot on the lower reaches of Pilgrim Street clearly depicts the poor living conditions in the oldest parts of Newcastle in the early twentieth century. There were a number of pockets of very crowded and dilapidated slums in and around this area of the Tyne. Children such as these could use anything they could get hold of to turn into toys, and the youngster in the foreground is holding a home-made skipping rope. As new business premises spread from Quayside up the slopes of Pilgrim Street a number of ancient houses were swept away. Subsequently the site was transformed into a motorway with the Swan House roundabout now occupying this area. The multi-storey office block in its centre is currently being demolished to make way for a hotel and luxury flats.

▽ A well-dressed little boy and girl play together on the street, quite oblivious to the other children around them. The location is the same spot on the lower reaches of Pilgrim Street as seen in the view above. The boy must have had affluent parents as most families could not afford the clothes he is wearing, and certainly not the expensive toy fire engine. Other children gaze enviously into the nearby shop window wishing they had the means to buy the goods on display, although it is possible that this is a posed photograph and they were given directions by the photographer.

△ Captioned 'A quaint corner in Newcastle', the building illustrated here was located between Dean Street and Pilgrim Street and built over the top of the deep valley of the Lort Burn, which ran down Side and across Sandhill to the Tyne. The steps are still in use today but the buildings have long since been demolished.

◁ Dean Street was originally built to provide easier access to Sandhill and Mosley Street at the upper end of the town. It was constructed across the Lort Burn between 1784 and 1789 by David Stephenson. The name Dean Street transpired from the dene that ran beneath it, described at the time as a 'vast nauseous hollow'.

On 26 September 1748 this house at the head of [th]e was the birthplace of Cuthbert Collingwood. He [ha]d an extremely successful career in the navy, [cu]lminating in him taking command of the fleet at [Tr]afalgar in 1805 when Nelson perished. A memoir [of] him, published two months after his death in the [M]ay 1810 edition of the *London Review*, recollected that [at] a very early age his genius indicated a propensity [to]ward a maritime life', adding that 'He adorned his [co]untry with glory, increased the security of its [in]habitants, and has left his fame of actions to speak [to] all nations'. On the centenary of his death in 1910 [th]ere was a grand civic procession from the old town [ha]ll to St Nicholas Cathedral where a wreath was laid [on] his bust. A similar ceremony took place at his [m]onument in St Paul's Cathedral in London. When [th]is postcard was produced at the start of the [tw]entieth century, the building was being used as a [se]cond-hand clothes shop. It was demolished very [sh]ortly afterwards to make way for Milburn House.

◁ Built over a period of three years commencing in 1902, Milburn House remains one of the city's most impressive and well-known buildings. In the nineteenth century this area was the site of the primary route into Newcastle and bustled with the activity of shoppers and traders. However, with the construction of the High Level bridge, the site lost its importance and rapidly declined, paving the way for this towering new structure. The first occupants of the new offices were shipping companies including P&O and Cunard. To highlight the building's close links with the shipping community, the floors were given letters rather than numbers, a practice in keeping with the decks on a ship.

▷ At the beginning of the twentieth century the area around Castle Garth was extremely dilapidated, with housing pressed alongside shops selling second-hand goods and very poor standards of sanitation. Castle Garth links the old castle and Black Gate to Castle Square, and this 1905 view looks towards St Nicholas Cathedral. A portion of the street sign for Dog Leap Stairs is visible above the street lamp. This is a very steep stairway providing a precarious short cut to Side. It also gives access to the Dog Leap Stairs antique shop at the foot of the stairs, a long-established shop which is still open today.

◁ From about 1760 Newcastle began to experien〈 pressure for more space from its growing populatio〈 and expanding industry. At the time the lower pa〈 of the old town had a number of steep, gloomy char〈 running down to Quayside. The confines of the ol〈 city wall and gates, among them Cowgate, we〈 becoming an increasing nuisance and causing traff〈 congestion. To lessen the problem the head 〈 Cowgate was widened and some of the surroundir〈 buildings removed to relieve the pressure.

Cowgate, Head of.
Broad Chare in 1912
Bits of Old Newcastle

A151. THE SIDE, NEWCASTLE ON TYNE

Seen here from Queen Street, Side is a long curved street which stretches from Quayside towards St Nicholas Cathedral, passing under the railway viaduct that spans both and Dean Street. Today only part of it remains, as the head of Side had to be demolished in order to make way for the construction of the High Level bridge. Deriving its name from its position to the 'side' of the castle, this area was once a centre of trade and commerce and the street acted as a vital city artery. McKenzie's description of it in 1827 still carries some relevance even today: 'Passing in the middle of The Side the ascent becomes very steep, and added to its extreme narrowness, and the dingy houses on each side, the passage is unconsciously gloomy and dangerous'. The offices and printworks of Andrew Reid's publishing company were housed here on the ground floor of Akenside House (foreground). Originally Reid's had premises in Pilgrim Street and also Grey Street. The company moved from Akenside House to Gallowgate in the mid-1920s when the approach road to the new Tyne bridge was under construction.

A fine 1921 view of Akenside Hill (also known as Butcher Bank), named after the poet Mark Akenside, with Side in the background. The Newcastle Arms pub is on the corner, marking the boundary between the two streets.

Akenside Hill in 1921
...ts of Old Newcastle

△ Many of the original architectural features of these wealthy merchants' homes in Sandhill can still be seen today. The street is said to have obtained its name because it was originally the site of a sandy hill when the tide was out, being covered by the Tyne the rest of the time. In the eighteenth century the area was adorned with stately buildings such as Newcastle's original town hall and guildhall. A statue of James II also stood here until a group of disgruntled locals tore it down and hurled it into the river. By the time this photograph was taken in the early 1900s, Sandhill had become a narrow, dark street lined with warehouses and shops. In the foreground at No. 34 are the premises of Bell & Dunn, a firm of ships' store merchants who later expanded into Nos. 36 and 38 before moving to 20 Broad Chare in the 1960s.

▽ Sandhill viewed from the approach road to the Swir bridge looking east. In the distance at No. 34 is th greengrocers business belonging to Miss E. S. Edminson; ne door is the long-established Cafe & Cocoa Rooms (also visib in the previous picture) and to its left the paint manufacturer shop of A. H. Davis Ltd. The house above the latter is that Bessie Surtees, a rich and socially prominent young lady wl married a man of 'low origins'. Her family frowned upc the marriage but locals hailed it as a triumph of romance ov status. Between Monday and Saturday the street bustled wi shoppers and traders, but on Sundays it was used for a qui different purpose. Newcastle's 'Speaker's Corner' w, situated here and every Sunday a wide range of political ar religious oratory was on offer.

Sandhill, Newcastle-on-Tyne.

The Swing bridge seen from the Gateshead side of the Tyne most 50 years after it was opened in 1876. Built by W. G. rmstrong & Co., the bridge is famed for its central moving an, a major feat of engineering. It is still operated today sing Armstrong's hydraulic machinery, although electric umps have replaced the original steam pumps. The major enefit of the bridge was that it allowed large seagoing vessels ccess to the upper reaches of the Tyne, and so encouraged dustrial development on both sides of the river beyond ewcastle and Gateshead, most notably at Elswick. The ntern tower of St Nicholas Cathedral is noticeable on the ft in this view, with the Moot Hall in the centre and the uildhall to the far right.

▽ Steam colliers, sturdy little single-funnelled steamers, helped to generate a great increase in coal shipments from the North-East, and by 1913 more than twenty million tons of coal and coke were being exported to London annually. This 1916 picture shows one of the many colliers to pass through the Swing bridge. Today, with the industrial decline of the region, the bridge is seldom seen open, but in the first half of the twentieth century it was extremely well-used. As a ship approached its captain would slow down and give three blasts on her steam whistle. The master on the bridge would answer with three corresponding blasts and then the captain would order one single blast in acknowledgement. The structure only took 90 seconds to open and was clearly an impressive design in its time, much like the newly opened neighbouring Millennium bridge.

◁ One of the old Swing bridge's famous faces was Thomas Ferrens, w[ho] had been born blind and partially disabled in 1841. Nicknamed 'Tom[my] on the bridge', he could be seen begging and scrounging, day in and d[ay] out, until his death on New Year's Day 1907. He ingeniously avoid[ed] prosecution by standing at the centre of the bridge, at the exact bor[der] between Newcastle and Gateshead. When approached by the police [he] would step from one side of the centre line to the other and hence out [of] the area of their jurisdiction, meaning that he was rarely apprehend[ed]. Photographed here shortly before his death, Tommy's demise was record[ed] as being attributed to 'apoplexy, accelerated by exposure to severe weat[her] and cold', hardly surprising considering he stayed out in all weathe[r]. He was renowned for showering colourful language on any passer-[by] who chose to ignore his plight and failed to give him a copper or two!

▽ The message on the reverse of this postcard reads: 'This is the Roy[al] Train crossing the High Level bridge'. King Edward VII and Que[en] Alexandra pulled into Newcastle Central station on the Royal Train [at] 11.30 a.m. on Tuesday 10 July 1906. The visit was described in the *Eveni[ng] Chronicle* as 'the consummation of a hope that had existed in the breasts [of] Novocastrians and Tynesiders for generations'. Great preparations h[ad] been made for the arrival: ropes of evergreens were stretched from colum[ns] to buildings, temporary metal frameworks were attached to tramway po[les] and lamp-posts and adorned with flower arrangements, and long stri[ps] of foliage entwined Grey's Monument. After a 21-gun salute Newcastle['s] mayor, Baxter Ellis, presented a cigarette box to the king and the que[en] received a pendant. The royal party then made their way to Armstro[ng] College which was officially opened by the king, before proceeding to t[he] Royal Victoria Hospital where a statue of Queen Victoria was unveile[d]. The day ended with a lunch reception at the Assembly Rooms where t[he] king said in his speech 'By the public spirit of your citizens you ha[ve] developed into a community of which every member may feel prou[d]'. Thousands of people witnessed the royal visit and all roads leading to t[he] city had to be closed because of congestion. Though it rained heavily [it] was reported that the poor weather did little to dampen the spirit of t[he] crowds.

Building the New Tyne Bridge. 8th. Feb. 1927 (1)

Local engineer T. M. Webster first proposed Newcastle's famous Tyne bridge in 1921, arguing that it was needed to augment the existing High Level bridge. Five tenders were submitted for its construction, and the lowest priced one, from Dorman Long & Co., Middlesborough, was accepted in December 1924. The company had previously been awarded the Sydney Harbour bridge project in Australia and this promoted their suitability as candidates as the two structures were so similar. Work on the bridge commenced in 1925 and after many buildings had been demolished, including five pubs, the foundations to support the new bridge were completed.

▽ A diagram of the construction of the Tyne bridge, reproduced from the souvenir brochure given to local schoolchildren on the occasion of its opening.

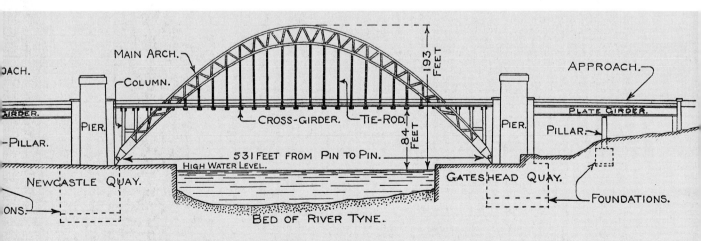

THE NEW BRIDGE OVER THE RIVER TYNE AT NEWCASTLE.

▽ By the time this photograph was taken on 5 May 1927, Tyneside's inhabitants were able to obtain their first impression of the grand scale of the new bridge, seen here already dwarfing the neighbouring Swing bridge to the west. The proprietors of the older bridge were staunchly opposed to the new structure as it would not only compete with them for toll revenue, but there had also been suggestions that the Swing bridge should eventually be demolished once its large neighbour was completed.

The New High Level Br

△ By early February 1928 the new Tyne bridge was beginning to take on its familiar shape. Many of the tension cables had been set in place and the twenty-ton cranes were positioned at the crown of the arch ready to complete their work. Sir William Joseph Noble described this stage as 'The steel arched hand of Newcastle stretching across father Tyne to clasp the outstretched hand of Gateshead'. Born in 1862, Noble played a leading role in the world of commercial shipping and in recognition of his services was made a baronet in 1921. He was given a peerage in 1930 on completion of five years' service to the Tyne Improvement Commission.

May 5th. 1927. (11)

By June 1928 the two separate halves of the arch had become one, and work to lay a suitable road surface had started. This put to bed the fears of some on the south of the Tyne who had been concerned about how their horses would cope scaling the arch in order to cross the river! Work had also commenced on the two towers, which had been designed as five-floor warehouses. Realising the towers would not be finished in time for the planned opening ceremony it was decided to concentrate all efforts on completing their exteriors, as the interiors could be finished at a later date. To this day the towers are still waiting to have their five floors put in place.

The completed Tyne bridge, seen here on 6 September 1928. Costing over £1 million to construct, its total length was 1,275 feet, of which 531 feet spanned the river. At its highest point it rose 193 feet above the Tyne and 7,000 tons of steel were used to build it. Even in the very beginning, electric lifts were fitted on the Newcastle side of the bridge to assist pedestrians to move from quay level to bridge height. Following completion, plans for a grand opening ceremony one month later were finalised. The Tyne bridge represents the heart and soul of Tyneside, best expressed by Jackie Milburn, Newcastle United's famous centre forward of the 1950s: 'The only time I'm really happy is when I come back over the Tyne bridge and smell the pit heaps. That's when I know I'm home.'

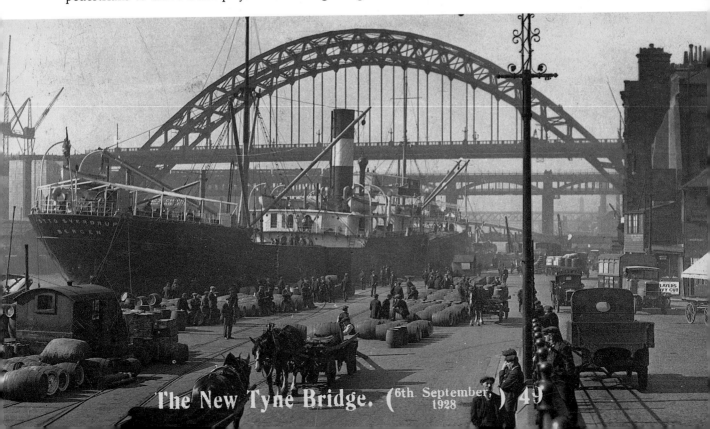

The New Tyne Bridge. (6th September, 1928) 49

OPENING OF THE TYNE BRIDGE, 10th, OCTOBER 1928, by
His Majesty The King.

△ King George V and Queen Mary were very welcome visitors when the Tyne bridge was opened on 10 October 1928. Accompanied by dignitaries from both sides of the river, including the Lord Mayor of Newcastle, Stephen Easten, and the Mayor of Gateshead, the official opening ceremony was a highly significant episode in the history of Tyneside and its people. The local paper, the *Evening Chronicle*, reported that 'Everywhere their Majesties were accorded a tumultuous welcome by densely packed crowds of cheering, flag waving citizens'. People had arrived at the bridge in the early hours, and thousands voiced their deafening appreciation of the event.

▽ Because of the area's significant economic decline at this period, a minority of people resented the king and queen's arrival on Tyneside and some in the crowd commented 'I bet they don't have empty bellies'. The king displayed his gravest sympathy for the decline, however, commenting in his speech that 'It is my earnest hope that this notable improvement in the facilities of transport may help bring back to your city that full tide of prosperity which your patience under recent difficulties so justly deserves'.

OPENING OF THE TYNE BRIDGE, 10th, OCTOBER 1928, by
His Majesty The King.

△ Though still in existence today, this photograph clearly shows that the Quayside's Sunday morning market is now a shadow of its former self, lacking the character and vibrancy that was once so prevalent. The streets were thronged each week with a largely male crowd, each dressed in their Sunday best complete with cap or boater, more likely than not only recently redeemed from the local pawnshop. The men would gather for a variety of amusements, including strongmen, artists, racing tipsters and a wide range of refreshments. Sadly, leather goods and mobile phone accessories are just about the market's only attractions today.

▽ A typical scene at the Quayside market in 1915, by which time it had been in existence for over 100 years. In 1873 Charleton wrote: 'On this portion of the Quay is held on Sundays a sort of fair. It is occupied by stalls of gaily covered awnings, mostly owned by Italian vendors of ice cream. The thirsty ones from the crowded Sandhill flock hither for their cold refreshment, which they diversify with ginger beer, lemonade, nuts, oranges and mussels. The quack doctor and the temperance and religious orders have also their places here.' Part of the railway line that ran the whole length of Quayside is visible at the bottom right-hand corner of the picture. This was laid by the North Eastern Railway Company in order to facilitate the growing traffic on the river in foodstuffs and general merchandise.

△ The Sunday market has always been a favourite venue for soapbox orators. This picture shows 'One-eyed Scottie' in full flow in 1905. He was a racing tipster who had a regular pitch and often dressed in jockey's silks. He invariably attracted a bunch of mug punters who eagerly awaited his next racing tip!

◁ The sight of masses of people rummaging for second-hand clothes bargains was a familiar one on Sunday mornings at the eastern outskirts of Newcastle Quayside Market. The market was known as Paddy's Market, and sellers used to turn up, come rain or shine, to try and earn some extra cash. Most of the clothes had been thrown out by city residents or bought for a small sum by the local rag and bone man, who called round the streets with his horse and cart shouting out for 'any rags and woollens', for which he was prepared to pay a small sum of ready cash. The old clothes would often find their way to Paddy's Market to be recycled at a profit.

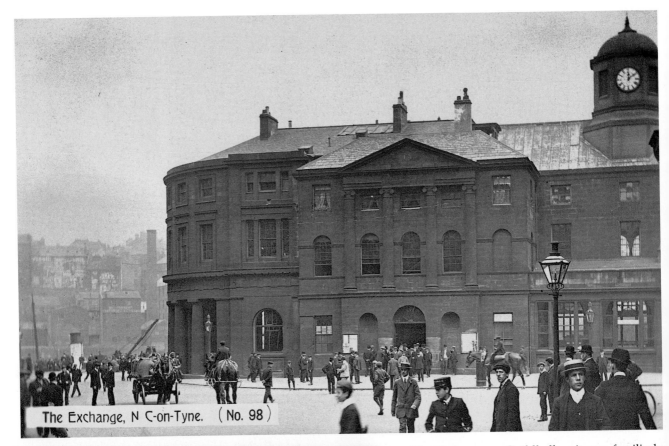

The Exchange, N C-on-Tyne. (No. 98)

△ The Exchange or Guildhall as it was familiarly known was used as the court of assize. From 1400 to 1881 Newcastle was both a town and county in its own right, separate from the county of Northumberland. Proceedings at assizes were opened in the Guildhall but the judge then proceeded to the Moot Hall to determine cases. The original Guildhall building was erected in the seventeenth century to plans drawn up by Robert Trollop and included features of both Renaissance and Gothic style architecture. The contract price was £2,000 but expenses accumulated at an alarming rate and the ultimate bill ran to £10,000. Extensive alterations followed after a fire in 1791, and the south elevation was reconstructed in 1809. In 1823 John Dobson was commissioned to design a new hall and Merchant Adventurers Courtroom (illustrated here). Below it stood the open colonnaded fish market, but in 1880 this was walled up and became a newsroom.

◁ Anthony Hall must have come from a reasonably well-off family as in the late 1880s he lived in Alexander Crescent in the wealthy suburb of Jesmond. By the end of the century he owned premises at 69 Quayside and 47 Side. He enjoyed over 50 years in business and is seen here standing with a distinct sense of pride at the entrance of his 'toilet saloon' at 36 Quayside in 1912. In reality this was a tobacconists shop, sandwiched between Customs House Chambers, a building housing several shipbroking companies, and the HM Customs House. Hall later moved to 32 Louvaine Terrace, Jesmond, near to his previous home. He had ceased trading at Quayside by 1953 when the Forster Tobacco Company Ltd. acquired these premises.

THIS IS ONE OF SLATER & Co.'s

TELEPHONE, 1229 OR 200
W. SLATER & Co.,
NEWCASTLE-ON-TYNE

△ Only the well-to-do and wealthy could afford to use this grand horse-drawn taxicab belonging to W. Slater & Co., photographed *c.*1913. The firm's main premises were in the portico of Central station, with a subsidiary branch in Haymarket Lane to the north of the city. By the 1960s the business had grown substantially and Slater's motor taxis were a very familiar sight on the streets of Newcastle. In addition to their taxi service, Slater's also offered funeral and wedding cars for hire, and most bizarrely the lease of a private ambulance.

▽ This Sentinel steam wagon belonged to the fleet of John Baxter & Co., local transport and storage contractors. Their head office was situated at 141 Quayside from where in the 1930s they offered the services of 'horse and motor haulage, general forwarding, and the warehousing of goods at reasonable rates'.

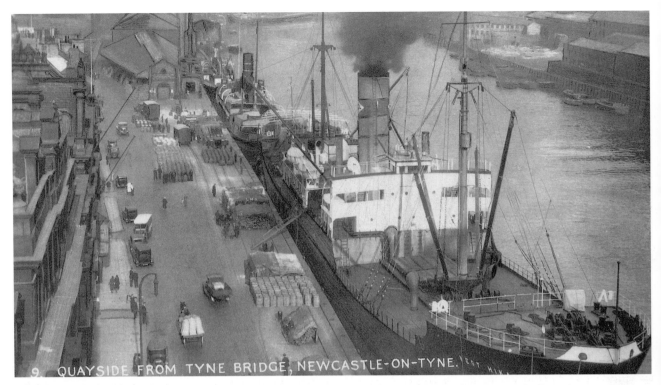

9 QUAYSIDE FROM TYNE BRIDGE, NEWCASTLE-ON-TYNE.

△ A busy quayside scene photographed from the Tyne bridge in 1934 with lorries and carts loading and unloading goods from several ships. The vessel *West Hika* (foreground) has just unloaded a number of crates which are piled up on the quay. The Tyne originally had no docking facilities and large ships could only take aboard their cargoes from keels in the lower reaches of the river. These smaller vessels were loaded from quaint wooden staithes up and down the river. The Victorian era heralded a vast transformation of the quayside, with the Tyne deepened and widened to improve its docking facilities. By the 1930s coal shipments on the Tyne had increased fourfold, and the vast tonnage of vessels using the port created a massive import and export trade.

▽ Goods from New Zealand being offloaded from the merchant ship *Fordsdale* at the quayside. On many occasions, especially when war prevented imports from coming into the country, quality fresh produce could not be found on the dinner tables of North-East households. In order to boost trade, Commonwealth countries sought every opportunity to publicise their goods and in this clearly posed photograph New Zealand butter is being heavily promoted. The caption on the postcard reads: 'New Zealand now sends regular monthly shipments of butter and cheese direct to Tyneside'.

△ The passenger steamer SS *Highlander*, owned by the Aberdeen, Newcastle & Hull Steam Co. Ltd. of Aberdeen, leaves the Tyne en route to Hull in 1923. The timetable took it from Aberdeen to Newcastle and Hull every Saturday, returning from Hull every Wednesday and Newcastle every Thursday.

◁ On 15 September 1928 in Newcastle Town Hall's concert hall, the presentation of 'a magnificent, glittering, sweet tongued silver bell to Britain's mightiest battleship, HMS *Nelson*' (*Evening Chronicle*) took place. Fired by local manufacturer Reid & Sons using 2,000 ounces of silver, the bell captured the public's imagination as it was seen as a permanent link between HMS *Nelson* and her birthplace on the Tyne. A great crowd gathered to watch the bell make its journey down Grainger Street on the limber of a field gun, which was drawn on drag ropes to the town hall where Captain Mayrick thanked Newcastle's inhabitants for 'this wonderful token of loving esteem, affection and goodwill for the *Nelson*'.

Official Japanese visit to Newcastle. 24/4/06. No.

△ Twenty-four officers of the Japanese warship *Kashima* visited Newcastle as guests of Mayor Alderman J. Baxter Ellis on 24 April 1906. A large crowd gathered at the quayside, silent but intrigued by the smart uniforms and smiling faces, to witness the party pass up Dean Street and along Mosley Street to the town hall where they were met by the *Kashima*'s Captain Ijichi. In the evening 150 of *Kashima*'s crew were given permission to remain ashore to attend St James' Park, where Newcastle United were playing against Stoke City.

▽ The crew of the Red Barns sub fire station in Crawhall Road photographed with their horse-drawn hose tender in the winter of 1909. Fireman Hardie is standing in the middle of this photograph and was the only full-time fireman at the station at that time, retiring from service in 1914. The other men were all auxiliaries.

◁ At 3.30 p.m. on 20 September 1906 the Tyne reportedly witnessed its 'most interesting launch ever seen' (*Evening Chronicle*) from the Wallsend shipyard of Swan, Hunter & Wigham Richardson. SS *Mauretania*'s christening ceremony was performed by the Dowager Duchess of Roxburghe. Some 760 feet long, and with a gross weight of almost 32,000 tons, her steel plates were held together with 4 million rivets – statistics that were in keeping with her position as the world's largest ship.

▽ The completed *Mauretania* creeps her way slowly along the Tyne. The distance from the waterline to the top of her funnels was 155 feet, almost as tall as the famous Grey's Monument in Newcastle, while her masts would have towered above St Nicholas Cathedral. Large crowds gathered to watch her as she sailed into the distance, with one brave individual scaling the heights of the great chimney stack by the river at Walker to obtain a bird's-eye view. A few false alarms meant that muffled cheers could be heard along the Tyne before her arrival, but when *Mauretania* came fully into view the crowds went into convulsions of excitement. The excitement was short-lived, however, as she was almost immediately obscured from view by the volumes of steam and smoke she produced.

LAUNCH OF THE S.S. MAURETANIA. (THE LARGEST SHIP IN THE WORLD) SEP. 20 1906.

Q.T.S.S MAURETANIA LEAVING THE TYNE

△ The Carpenters' Tower was erected during the eight-year period from 1299 to 1307 and got its current name because the Carpenters' Company made alterations to it in 1716. It has been known by a variety of different names over the years, including the Sallyport Tower and Wall Knoll Tower. Originally the tower formed part of the town walls and today is the only one of the city's medieval gateways to survive. In this 1912 view the lower part of the building is occupied by Henry Pooley & Son Ltd., weighing machine manufacturers, and there is an advertising hoarding publicising land for sale by Mather & Dickinson 'in lots to suit purchasers'.

▽ Sandgate was one of Newcastle's worst slums. For the unskilled or infirm, the only homes available were in overcrowded slum areas such as this one and others at Quayside and Sandgate, where the poverty and deprivation was amongst the worst in the country. Often up to four families shared a single room in lodging houses; most rooms had very little natural light and no proper cooking or sanitation facilities. The shop of James Lilley Bainbridge, who was a ship and general smith by trade, is visible at No. 15 Sandgate. Mr Bainbridge conducted his business here for over 50 years from the early twentieth century onwards. His company manufactured cargo and coal gins, engineers' and snatch blocks, railway hooks, crane hooks and self-lubricating blocks and gins. The Lord Nelson Inn was close by at 11 Sandgate.

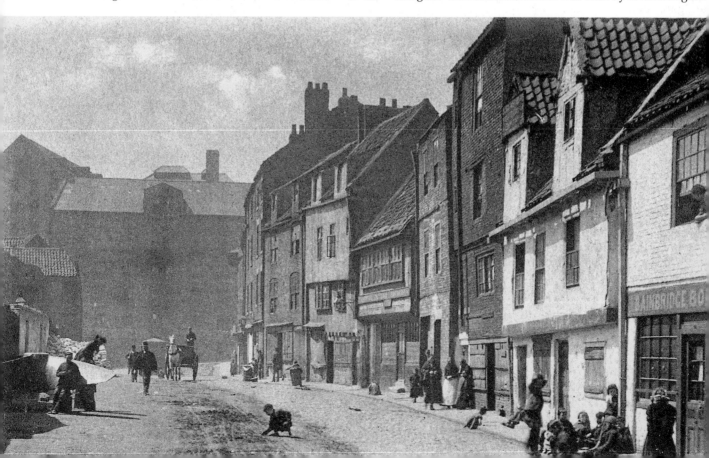

△ Reproduced from a postcard captioned 'Music in the slums', this picture shows some welcome entertainment for the inhabitants of Sandgate being provided by itinerant musicians in the late nineteenth century. Children in torn and ragged clothes, many of them barefoot, watch and listen intently to the entertainment. Child suffering and destitution was prevalent in Sandgate with diseases such as consumption and whooping cough rife, exacerbated by poor housing conditions.

How to make the best of a humdrum existence. A bedraggled, forlorn young boy drags a couple of very young children along the pavements of Sandgate in an uncomfortable wooden box on wheels with a piece of rope to steer it. The postcard is entitled 'A primitive pram'. Sent to a Mr M. Young of Hoyle, Shipley & Hoyle, 8 Westgate Road, the message on the back reads: 'This is the very latest in prams, although it does not look very comfortable. Hope you will be able to afford something nicer than this for the dear little twins.'

△ The New Bridge Street goods station seen in 1920 from New Bridge Street. The latter is a continuation of Blackett Street running eastwards from the city centre, and was named after the 'new bridge' which was built in 1812 to span the Pandon Burn. The bridge was eventually demolished when the burn was filled in. From 1850 the south side of New Bridge Street was occupied by the Trafalgar goods station, which was eventually pulled down and replaced by this new structure, which opened on the north side of the street on 2 January 1907. The goods station was subjected to constant bombing during the Second World War and was very badly damaged in 1941. It lay in ruins for many years before finally being demolished in 1986. Warner Bros. multiplex cinema now occupies the site. The advertisement just to the left of centre has been placed by D. Gillis & Co. extolling the public to cross the (Byker) bridge to buy their house furnishings.

▽ In 1902 the North Eastern Railway decided to electrify its suburban services on Tyneside, prompted by the fact that it was losing passengers to the electric tramways. The first train on the NER's new electric service left New Bridge Street passenger station (on the south side of the street) for Benton on 29 March 1904 at 12.50 p.m. It was painted in a distinctive livery of bright red and cream. The chairman of the NER, Lord Ridley, carried out the opening ceremony. The new train took only eleven minutes to complete the journey to Benton, stopping at Jesmond, West Jesmond and Gosforth along the way. This new service was a valuable addition to the city's transport network, operating reliably at fifteen minute intervals. When it was first introduced many people made the journey just to experience this latest form of travel.

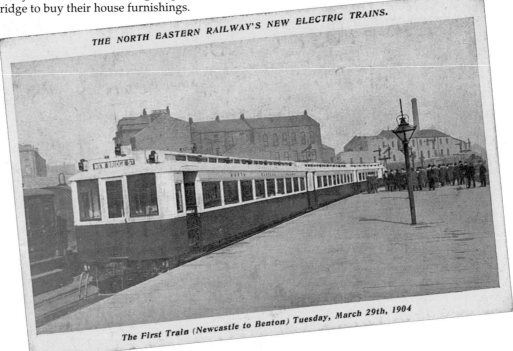

THE NORTH EASTERN RAILWAY'S NEW ELECTRIC TRAINS.

The First Train (Newcastle to Benton) Tuesday, March 29th, 1904

NEW BRIDGE RY. STATION. N/C.   ARMATAGE,

△ This photograph shows the full extent of the New Bridge Street passenger station site during building and reconstruction work in 1908.

▷ Angus Watson & Co. came to prominence in the early 1920s as importers, and later became renowned as canned goods merchants with premises at No. 5 City Road. By the 1950s the company had become Pelling, Watson & Green Ltd. This advert for their Skippers brand of sardines dates from around 1950. The company employed very vigorous techniques to encourage customer loyalty, and the text on the reverse of this postcard invites shoppers to join in their 'profit-sharing scheme'. It goes on to explain that 'in exchange for labels taken from the Angus Watson [range of] ready-to-serve foods', a variety of gifts could be collected. In this case a crystal cut-glass powder bowl 'which will add a note of refinement to any boudoir table' was on offer. Over 200 other 'valuable' gifts were to be found in their illustrated catalogue. The factories eventually became part of the John West group.

Skippers

Oh Mother!

H. Dady, whose cart carries the wording 'Potato Salesman', but who is described on the boxes he is sitting on as a Banana Merchant, had a very long-established fruit and vegetable business with branches at several locations in the city (one of which was at New Bridge Street goods station). In the 1920s he also had premises at 10 High Friars Street and at St Andrews Street in the heart of the city's fruit and vegetable market. When the market was demolished in the late 1960s to make way for the Eldon Square shopping centre it transferred to the Team Valley Trading Estate in Gateshead.

△ Shieldfield came to the fore during England's Civil Wars in the mid-seventeenth century when a great fort stood here as part of the city's defences. It played a crucial role during the siege of 1644. For many years Shieldfield was used as a place of recreation, although the only part of the original recreation grounds now remaining is Shieldfield Green, a small triangular grassed area near Christ Church. Some of the area's oldest houses are seen in this picture.

▽ There was considerable resistance to women participating in sport in the early 1900s, and cycling was one of only a few activities they could enjoy without being frowned upon. This early twentieth century postcard shows Joseph Appleby accompanied by his son and three daughters on a variety of different sized bikes. The Applebys were in business as fish and paper merchants from 1907 at 77 Shield Street in Shieldfield, but moved ten years later to nearby Falconer Street, sharing the premises there with Miss S. Gardener, also a fish merchant. A succession of fish dealers occupied the premises at 77 Shield Street and by the outbreak of World War II a Mrs Murray was the proprietor. The reverse of this postcard reveals that Joseph Appleby was 'Agent for J. D Fellows & Co.'s Batter Colouring', and also 'Sole representative of Messrs. Mabbotts, Ltd., Manufacturers of Fish Friers Outfittings'.

Joseph Appleby, Shieldfield, Newcastle, and his four Children, all Clever Cyclists.

MEGGIE
6 yrs. (World Challenger at 3 yrs.)

ELSIE
10 years.

J. APPLEBY
Father.

HANNAH
2 years.

JOE
4 years.

△ A funeral scene from the early 1920s with a horse-drawn hearse waiting outside the shop of Andrew Docherty while the coffin is loaded and wreath-carrying mourners assemble. Mr Docherty spent 40 years in business as a furniture broker and dealer. He had begun his working life in 1895 as a furniture broker at 16 Shield Street and ten years later expanded into premises at Nos. 36 and 38 in the same street. By 1922 he was describing himself as a furniture dealer, with shops at 13 and 38 Shield Street, off Shieldfield Green. He lived above the premises at No. 38.

▽ Robert Greer & Co.'s livery stable and commission yard at 3 Sandyford Road, seen on a postcard sent in 1913. Mr Greer had acquired the premises from T. Dawson at the end of the nineteenth century, after which he set about establishing his 'old times livery stable' from where he offered 'good loose boxes' and advertised 'special attention given to breaking young horses'. In the 1930s he shared his stables with A. Dagliesh, a horse shoer, and at this time converted his business into a more lucrative riding school. There was a clear sign of changing times in the early 1950s when Robson & Everard Co., automobile agents, moved into the building, and by the end of the decade Greer's was no longer in business in the area.

The company of William J. Watson had their 'Tyne Electrical Confectionery Works' in Union Road, Byker from the early twentieth century. The firm remained in business there until the early 1960s, although the works were generally known as Watson's toffee works from the 1930s onwards. The former name of the company perhaps emphasised that it was a modern concern, with its machinery powered by electricity. In 1909 they were advertising their new line of Watson's Butter Milk Toffee, priced 2d for four ounces at the time. Retailers could opt to try a sample 4 lb tin on a sale or return basis by way of an introductory offer.

A quiet view of Byker bridge in 1910. Built at a cost of £50,000 using private finance and opened in 1878, locals had to pay for the privilege of using it by coughing up an unpopular toll. A handsome profit was made by the bridge owners when Newcastle City Council bought it for the sum of £107,500 in 1890. It had been expected that the toll would be abolished immediately, but the council did not act until five years later as they wanted to recoup some of their expenditure on the acquisition. The bridge crossed the Ouseburn and by the time this picture was taken the area was becoming heavily industrialised.

W.J. WATSON'S

WATSON'S BUTTER MILK TOFFEE

Butter Milk Toffee

BYKER, NEWCASTLE-ON-TYNE

IT'S WATSON'S.

BYKER BRIDGE, NEWCASTLE.

A.S.T.V.W. VESTIBULE CAR 1911
PRESENTED N/C with COMPLIMENT's COMMITTEE'S

H ROSS President

H Goodhead . Sec=

Councillor (later Alderman) Rodgers reported to Newcastle Council in 1911 that 'I am a great believer in corporations owning and working their own tramways run on business lines', considering that the travelling public [should be] supplied with proper accommodation and facilities'. Newcastle vestibule tramcar (Class E Balcony) No. 193 came into service that year having been presented to Newcastle Corporation. Class E tramcars were known as 'Maids of all work' as they could be found anywhere on the tramway system. By 1914 tram routes radiated from the city in every direction. There were 63 miles of track and 211 tramcars covering a total distance of 5 million miles a year and carrying 58 million passengers. This postcard was sent on Christmas Eve 1911 by H. Goodhead (right) to Mr R. Brewster, Motorman, Byker Car Sheds, wishing him the compliments of the season. Motorman was the title that tram drivers went by.

Councillor Rodgers was also keen to see 'that good conditions of labour are given to all our workers', and supported that claim by awarding a starting wage of 26 shillings a week for tram conductors. Some 600 conductors benefited from what was regarded as a good reward at the time. Here a group of seven tramcar drivers and conductors pose proudly for the camera on the exit platform of a tram. Ultimately the number of tramway workers totalled 1,100, with the majority of conductors identified by odd numbers on their uniform, while motormen had even numbers. In 1926 the blue piping on their tunics was replaced by red piping.

POST CARD.

FOR CORRESPONDENCE.   ADDRESS TO BE WRITTEN HERE

HALF-
PENNY
STAMP.

ALL TICKETS READY PLEASE

T. JONES, NEWCASTLE-ON-TYNE.

Reprinted by permission of the "EVENING MAIL."

And last, but not least is our cheerful friend, with the melodious voice, the singing Tram Inspector.

"ALL TICKETS READY PLEASE."

(OR, THE MUSICAL TRAM INSPECTOR).
Newcastle-on-Tyne Corporation Tramways.

* * *

Tram Inspector Jones,
With his sweet dulcet tones,
Makes the passengers smile
As he sings all the while,
" All tickets ready please ! "

The new rag-time song
Is going very strong,
But Jones will not alter,
He sings without falter,
" All tickets ready please ! "

We all know his voice,
And the song of his choice,
We hear every day,
As he sings his glad lay,
" All tickets ready please ! "

New songs of the stage,
They may be all the rage,
Though none of them beating,
T. Jones' glad greeting,
" All tickets ready please ! "

May he be with us long,
Just to sing his old song,
For like carols that cheer,
Don't we all like to hear,
" All tickets ready please ! "

May he never retire,
Or ascend up higher,
With the angels to sing,
That most beautiful thing,
" All tickets ready please ! "

In the better land,
At the gate he will stand,
Checking tickets again,
With the same old refrain,
" All tickets ready please ! "

COPYRIGHT.

▷ The front and reverse of a pre-First World War postcard showing a caricature of tram inspector Jones, famed for singing while he worked. The lyrics appear to have been written by his fans, rather than the inspector.

▽ Photographed in 1952 at the works of Domestos Ltd., this fleet of motor vans advertise Stergene, a liquid disinfectant. Along with Stergene, the company made Domestos and insecticide at their College Works in Albion Row. The motor engineering department, body building department and advertising department had their premises at the St Anns Works. This postcard was sent by the company's advertising department to inform a customer when one if its window dressers would be calling at their shop to set up a window display.

△ When this photograph was taken in the early years of the twentieth century, the population of the parish of St Lawrence, a suburb in the Walker area to the east of Newcastle, was around 10,000. St Lawrence was a poor parish, made up mainly of unskilled shipworkers living in crowded slum conditions down on the edge of the Tyne. In 1909, in order to try and improve living conditions, Newcastle Corporation built two-storey blocks of tenement housing consisting entirely of single room dwellings. The corporation also owned the Sanatorium Quay at St Lawrence. Two privately-owned ferry boats provided a cross-river ferry service from Walker to Hebburn at regular intervals.

▽ Launched in 1913 and completed in May 1914, the *Aquitania* was built for the Cunard Line by John Brown & Co., Clydebank. The ship had facilities for approximately 600 first class, 600 second class, and 2,000 third class passengers. During her years in service she steamed 3 million miles, carried 1.2 million passengers and crossed the Atlantic 475 times. At the beginning of the First World War she was requisitioned by the government and converted to an armed merchant cruiser. She proved too big to be practical for this purpose, and was later used as a troopship during the Dardanelles campaign, then as a hospital ship for most of the period until 1917, returning to regular service with Cunard in June 1920 after a refit at the Tyneside yard of Armstrong Whitworth & Co. (who converted her from coal to oil fuel). *Aquitania* was again requisitioned by the government as a troopship during the Second World War, remaining so until 1948. In 1950 she was sold for breaking up at Gareloch in Scotland.

The "Aquitania" at Walker. 3447

△ Pandon Temperance AFC were members of the Newcastle United Free Churches Amateur Football League, which was instituted in 1901. They played their fixtures at High Pitt Farm, St Anthony's in the Walker area of Newcastle. The club secretary, Mr T. Scott, resided at 2 Wansbeck Street. The team usually played in either light and dark blue or red and white jerseys, although in this photograph of the 1909–10 line-up they are wearing plain strips. In April 1922 one of their players, Mr T. Burlinson, represented an England church eleven (playing in the black and white colours of Newcastle United) against Glasgow in an intercity match at Cathkin in front of 2,000 spectators. Burlinson was a pure individual, renowned for his tricky runs in a most enterprising forward line, and was outstanding throughout the match. His only blemish was shooting narrowly wide from the best chance of the game. The match ended in a disappointing 0–0 draw.

▽ If a reminder of the dangerous nature of work in the North East's shipyards was needed, then Walker's accident hospital should suffice. Seen here during the First World War, it was founded by Charles Mitchell and opened by Newcastle's mayor, James Morrison. It was the very first cottage hospital in the north of England, and shipyard workers paid membership subscriptions which acted as an insurance policy against work-related injuries. After the Second World War, with the focus shifting to national welfare provision, the NHS took over the running of the hospital. They renamed it Walker Park Hospital, a name it retained until its closure in 1976.

ACCIDENT HOSPITAL, WALKER.

MODEL YACHT 40
WALKER PARK

On 25 March 1888 twenty acres of land forming part of the Scrogg House Farm were leased to the Walker local board for the sum of £10 a year on the condition that they would spend £2,000 improving the land as a park. The work took three years to complete and on 3 August 1891 Mr T. Crawford, who was chairman of the city council, officially inaugurated Walker Park. The new park boasted a lake, tennis courts, football and cricket pitches, pavilions, statues and a bandstand. In more recent decades it fell into serious decline and by the 1980s badly needed improving. Norman Stockdale initiated a competition to design a new park in 1983, and this was won by Walker School. Walker Park was reopened by the Rt. Hon. Neil Kinnock on 27 May 1988. The cost of returning it to its former glory was £500,000.

▽ Byker Street post office was on the corner of Welbeck Road and Westbourne Street, and the postmaster was Mr D. Cowie when this photograph was taken in the early 1920s. Note the young boy perilously selling the local evening paper in the middle of the road. Most boys cherished hopes of a paper round, and the lucky ones were allocated one in a better-off area where they could make some extra money from tips. Many would hand over their earnings to their parents to help the family finances.

Welbeck Road, Walker. 4978

Shopkeepers in working class areas such as Walker needed to be astute businessmen and extremely hard-working to survive. They served communities which lived on the breadline and often had to offer credit or lose vital trade. Independent shops faced stiff competition from the co-operative movement which had three million members by 1914 and offered a rapidly increasing range of goods. Retailers hit back by pointing out that the co-op dividend, whereby members received anything up to 25 percent of the value of their purchases back by way of a dividend, was in fact their own money simply being given back to them as a proportion of what they had initially paid. The leather goods and bootmakers shop belonging to Francis Park was situated at the corner of Church Street and Welbeck Road. Mr Park lived nearby at No. 126 Welbeck Road. The two neighbouring shops were Miss Isabella Gatenby's milliners and fancy drapers, and Agnes Roscoe's general dealers and fruiterers.

Mrs Elizabeth E. Marley, posing in the doorway of her shop at 128 Welbeck Road in 1912. By 1928 the business had moved to 574 Welbeck Road. Clothing shops such as this catered for working class needs and the clothes would probably be recycled several times. Shopkeepers often lived above their premises, and in the clothing industry would usually offer a sewing, repair and make-up service. Almost everything on sale would have a local customer in mind, and Mrs Marley would have been a well-known figure in the local community.

△ Neat, regimented terraced houses in Sunningdale Avenue seen here in the early years of the First World War shortly after they had been built. The roads and some of the pavements had not been completed when the postcard was produced. Sunningdale Avenue branches off Welbeck Road opposite St Albans RC Primary School. Local children are standing on the unfinished road waiting to be captured on camera, presumably a non-school day!

▽ The imposing police buildings in Walker are shown here shortly after they opened in 1908. Situated on the corner of Wharrier Street and Rochester Street, they cost only £9,000 to construct. There was a great deal of attention to detail in the architecture and the figures above the entrance can be identified as Justice, Truth and Death. Originally it was intended that a fire station of a similar magnitude should be built alongside, but this plan never came to fruition.

△ David Henry Allan resided at 55 Avison Street and worked as a joiner in the early years of the twentieth century. In 1909 his shopfitters premises were situated on the north side of Park Place in Prudhoe Street; here managers, workers and a young apprentice pose for a photograph, along with the company cat. Mr Allan moved his business to Bells Court in Pilgrim Street in the mid-1950s, forming a limited company with his sons. The business continued trading into the late 1960s.

▽ This gathering of men dressed in military, police and Yeoman of the Guard uniforms with a banjo-playing butcher or two provides forceful evidence of hunger among Newcastle's poorer children in the late nineteenth and earl twentieth century. Strikes often caused much hardship an hunger, and it was not unusual for a local entrepreneur to fun a special morning breakfast for poor children. As a result o newspaper publicity, public support followed and throughou the period of the campaign local firms, societies and privat individuals donated funds to ensure that the children wer fed. This crowd, comprising the Poor Children Breakfas Committee, are most likely in fancy dress expressly to rais funds. The photograph was taken outside a pub in the Walke and the placard reads: 'Walker Distress, we are feeding dail 300 poor children'.

POOR CHILDREN BREAKFAST, COM.

△ Folk dancing on Tyneside has been described as 'a halfway house between Scottish and English influences, which make it unique', and the largest collections of mining songs in the country are attributed to North-East dances. The most famous form of North-East dance is the sword dance, where five men interlock swords to form a star. The symbolism of this evolves from the mining communities' dependence on mates (Geordie narras), represented by the interlocking swords. Folk dancing was an activity that could be enjoyed by all classes; it was free and an expression of community spirit. There were regular competitions between communities, which provoked friendly rivalry. A great deal of attention was paid to the costumes as each member of the club had to look immaculate, as illustrated here by the men and women of the East End Folk Dance Club, photographed in July 1927.

▽ This advert for the Anglo–Swedish Electric Welding Company dates from the 1930s. The firm specialised in the welding of boilers and high pressure vessels, and boasted 'repairs carried out under strict supervision, and to the satisfaction of the leading Insurance Companies and Classification Societies'. The Newcastle branch of the company was managed by K. Petersen, and had its premises above the Locomotive Inn in Glasshouse Street.